We Volunteered.

We Volunteered.

A BIOGRAPHY OF CARL ROBERT RUSE
SURVIVOR OF THE BATAAN DEATH MARCH
AND
PRISONER OF THE JAPANESE, 1942-1945

TIMOTHY C. RUSE

Washington, DC

First printing, 2010.
12.12.13 revision with Afterword.

Library of Congress Cataloging-in-Publication Data:

Library of Congress Control Number: 2010918006

Ruse, Timothy C., 1983-

Hard Cover ISBN-10   0-615-39332-2
Hard Cover ISBN-13   9780615393322
Paperback ISBN-10   0-615-39363-2
Paperback ISBN-13   9780615393636

For Holden Carl, Samuel Fount, and Sadie Jane;
For Michael and Steve;
For the Descendants of Carl Ruse;
Those with us, and those still to come.

CONTENTS

PREFACE

   This is the story of my Grandfather, Carl Robert Ruse, and his experiences leading up to and during the Second World War. I first "interviewed" him as a high-school senior for a Social Studies project. The idea to compile all of this material on his life came to me the year I became a father, only four years after he passed away. This work was done for my sons and for all of the descendants of my grandfather. I wish you had met him, and I want you to know this story. Sometimes I'll see you standing outside with your hands behind your back the way he did, just observing, and I know I'm watching a piece of him, still moving. Sometimes you will look up at an airplane flying over with pursed lips and one eye squinted just slightly, and I'll see him then too. And someday, I expect to see him in the way you carry out your life with a stubborn determination, honor, loyalty, hard work, and thankfulness.

   When I started this work, I would listen to and read the narrative accounts of his story, I noticed that at times he would tell a longer version of his story, and at other times, a shorter version.

Sometimes, he would focus on more detail in the beginning, and wind it up quickly in the end. There were always details that came into the story each time that might not have made it into a recording of another "telling" of the story. So it was at this time that I decided to work to compile all of these narratives together into one concise story.

Once this was completed, I had a basis from which to begin learning about different events, places, and people, and the project grew from there much further than I had ever initially intended. What started as a narrative became a narrative with a lot of footnotes. It was this narrative that formed the basic outline of this book, which I have researched and expanded upon within. I'm putting my name on this work not to take credit for it, but to take responsibility for the contents within. I took facts from many sources and direct accounts given by other soldiers and prisoners who were in the same places at the same time, from letters written, family history, and other memoirs by men who were there in the attempt to tell a more whole and concise story.

The content of this story is difficult and violent, and yet, as Carl Ruse once said to me, the most violent and appalling events of his war stayed in the Philippines. Some things were just too awful to repeat. This book was written with that context in mind. The use of the word "Jap" should raise an eyebrow as a slur in this present day with sixty years of separation from World War II, but implied a different meaning during its wartime context. William J. Dunn, an American broadcast war correspondent for CBS who covered the Pacific War from day one, expressed this idea well when he prefaced his memoir by saying:

> *"When is a Japanese a "Jap?"*
>
> *That's easy! It's when he's flying an enemy plane, occupying an enemy bunker, pacing the bridge of an enemy warship or merely trying to eliminate you from this earth.*
>
> *Since World War II I have twice lived in Japan and have visited the country several times. For the purpose of setting the record straight, I must report that in all that time I never really met a "Jap"* (Dunn 1988)

❖

I have to announce my gratitude to my dear wife for allowing me to invest my time in this project over a long period. I should also acknowledge Mark Lampman whose social studies class at Permian High School cultivated a greater appreciation for history in me. It was in his class that I did a first "interview" of my Grandfather on his wartime experiences; this was less than three years prior to his death. Over the years, I had heard numerous fragments of his story while perhaps sitting around the Thanksgiving table, on a fishing trip, or driving across Texas to a high-school football game on some Friday night; all of which left me with a spotty and censored idea of what he had experienced, but this opportunity to have him sit and tell his entire story to me was one of the most meaningful experiences in this epoch of my life.

I would also acknowledge Dr. Doug Thomas at Hardin-Simmons University who taught me the value of quality work and learning for learning's sake. Dr. Bob Barnes also of Hardin-Simmons introduced me to the life, works, and philosophy of Viktor Frankl, whose ideas were present in my mind as I worked on this project as they are frequently in my day to day. Finally, I must acknowledge Lillian Brown whom I knew from Georgetown University who told me "You owe it to the world and to your children to finish this project." Her directness and confidence lit a fire under me to get this project done.

When working on this project, I relied heavily on the great work of researchers who have done an enormous body of work on this subject. Two books by William H. Bartsch (*Doomed at the Start* & *December 8, 1941*) were outstanding resources, and provide some of the most comprehensive and thorough descriptions of conditions leading up to and during the surrender of forces in the Philippines. Mr. Bartsch allowed me to view his massive body of research and also introduced me to Jim Zobel, Archivist at the Douglas MacArthur Memorial in Norfolk, Virginia who was a great help with my research there. I also thank the staff at the National Archives in Washington DC for their assistance. Additionally, I would like to again thank my wife, Meagan for being the first reviewer of the final draft of this text, and to my old friend Gabriel Prado for his review of the text and invaluable advice.

❖

I hope I've written this in a way that would be a tribute to the hardships my grandfather suffered, and that the proverbs of his life are passed on. Without his endurance and survival, I would not have happened. Today, as I complete this project, I am twenty-seven years, five months, and one day old. When my grandfather stepped off of a ship in Manila on November 1st, 1941 into what would be a burning warzone only days later, he was twenty-seven years, five months and four days old. There will be nothing that will happen to me today that will even compare. I can complain about nothing. My greatest concerns are trivial in comparison; my life is good.

PROLOGUE

It was September of 1931 when Secretary of State Henry Stimson under President Hoover wrote in his diary: "Trouble has flared up again in Manchuria. The Japanese, apparently their military elements, have suddenly made a coup." This 1931 trouble was instigated by Army officers who wanted a war of conquest, and to themselves be more powerful than the Japanese Cabinet. By the end of 1931, the Japanese Army had taken over Manchuria despite protests of officials in Tokyo.[1] This was a sign of how in the years to come, the Army would shape the direction of the Japanese nation. America's rejection of this Japanese acquisition of Manchuria was an unforgiveable action in the eyes of the Japanese, whose citizens were heavily invested in the region, and saw themselves as colonizers rather than conquerors. The League of Nations condemned the act, causing Japan to quit the league. In what became known as the "Stimson Doctrine", the declaration was made; the U.S. would not recognize any territorial arrangements forcefully imposed upon China.[2]

In 1937, the Japanese Army invaded China, and then joined the Axis powers in September 1940, catching Washington by surprise. At the time, Japan was winning significant victories in China, and once again, the Japanese government had been brought down and controlled by the military. By 1941 the Army had occupied French Indo-China after France had fallen to Nazi Germany, and could not protect an interest in Asia. President Franklin Delano Roosevelt responded by banning the export of gasoline and iron and steel scraps to Japan. The move did nothing to slow Japan's expansions at the time, and only further aggravated the diplomatic climate. Yet, in Japan, the embargo was a difficult blow. The Japanese people consumed twelve-thousand tons of oil each day and had only two years of reserves. If the Japanese military were going to take aggressive action against the U.S., they would need to act soon, while the U.S. and allies were occupied with Germany in Europe. The likelihood of a confrontation with the west could only build as during the next year the U.S. and Japan traded actions that would do nothing to quiet the other, yet did everything to further provoke the opposite side.[3]

Without petroleum imports, Japanese industries dependent on foreign oil would be nearly paralyzed "in less than a year," and the navy would be disabled within two years. These dire circumstances caused something of a panic in Tokyo.[4]

General Hideki Tōjō, was a key contributor to the Japanese plan of forceful expansion. Tōjō was a short, bald man, with round eyeglasses and a mustache. He was a supporter of alliances with Germany and Italy, and after Japan joined forces with these nations, he became Minister of War. During the following year, the Imperial Army continued movements down the Asian mainland, threatening American, Dutch, and British interests. In response, American Secretary of State, Cordell Hull, demanded that Japan withdraw from the Chinese mainland and Indo-China. In answer, on September 6th, Imperial policymakers made a decision to go to war if negotiations failed.[5] Japanese Prime Minister Prince Fumimaro Konoye, who wished to prevent war, was given a month to reach common ground with the U.S. If an agreement to lift the embargo could not be reached by October 10th, armed forces would begin moving south.[6] When no solution had been arrived at by October 16th, Konoye resigned.

Japanese Emperor Hirohito, hoping for a peaceful solution turned to war minister Tōjō to form a new government, reviewing all issues again, and to begin preparing for war.[7] Tōjō immediately accepted the Emperor's request; he was already paranoid of American intentions and was encouraged by the conquests that Hitler was making in Europe. By November, Japan was preparing for combat.[8]

It was Tōjō who stiffened the resolve of other military officials towards taking the drastic step of attacking the west. The Commander in Chief of the Imperial Navy, Isoroku Yamamoto was condemned when he told Admirals that Japan could not defeat the United States in a long war, and therefore should not attack the Dutch East Indies, yet his recommendation was not received well. Yamamoto conceived the idea of an operation that would immobilize the United States for one year, and allow the Japanese to achieve sizable victories before attempting a negotiated settlement; if the war were to drag out longer, it would not end well for Japan.

The result of this plan was the bombing of Pearl Harbor, which was previously thought to be "impregnable" by FDR, the army, and navy. When it was over, eighteen U.S. vessels and one-hundred seventy-five aircraft had been destroyed, with another one-hundred fifty-nine damaged; the ships, anchored in rows in the harbor, and planes had been lined up wing-to-wing on the airstrip making them simple target.[9] An attack from Japan was not a surprise to the president, yet, an attack on Pearl Harbor was a staggering shock.

The Japanese Army and Navy won victories as predicted by Yamamoto, and for six months the Japanese ruled the Pacific. With few resources available for their defense, Singapore, Bataan and Corregidor fell. It was not until the battle at Midway, that America began to turn the tide in the Pacific. Japanese codes had been broken, and an enormous defeat was achieved. In June of 1942, the Japanese Navy suffered substantial losses, however, out of fear, the few that knew, as Yamamoto did, that a fatal wound had been suffered, did not speak up about the country's desperate situation. By this time, Japanese control of the Pacific was shrinking, and forces were being pushed back to their home islands. Near the end of the war, Tōjō was forced to resign and retired in seclusion to his home.[10]   By this time Japanese war efforts in the Pacific were desperate.   Suicide attack units composed of Zero fighters loaded with bombs were being organized to attack American aircraft carriers.

Meanwhile, American prisoners of war were dying of starvation and being killed daily, all while being used for slave labor to support the futile war efforts of a brutal Japanese army that showed no value for human life; neither its own nor that of its enemies.

CHAPTER I

WE VOLUNTEERED

This generation of Americans has come to realize, with a present and personal realization, that there is something larger and more important than the life of any individual or of any individual group -- something for which a man will sacrifice, and gladly sacrifice, not only his pleasures, not only his goods, not only his associations with those he loves, but his life itself.

Franklin Delano Roosevelt
Fireside Chat
February 23rd, 1942

Carl Ruse sat in an open box car on a freight train rolling southwest somewhere out of Enid, Oklahoma. Only a few hours earlier he had been sitting in a high school classroom. Being on the move was nothing new, but this time was different. Ruse had been born in Robinson, Illinois on the 29th of May, 1914, and his parents separated not long after. Since then he had moved plenty of times, changing hometowns and schools sometimes every couple of years. He lived with his Dad, Edward, and younger sister Ruth most of the time as they followed his Dad's work in the oil field wherever it would have them. Their hard-working and transient lifestyle had carried them all over the State of Texas and parts of Oklahoma, attending whatever schools were here and there.

Most recently, Carl had landed in Enid with his sister, mother and her husband. The stock market had taken the plunge in the previous year, and work was hard to find. It was 1930 and he was sixteen years old.

"I'll be at your house after school at about six o'clock. Be ready, because we're hopping the freight train and headed out west to California," said a friend at school just that afternoon. "I had thought he was joking," said Ruse. "...until he showed up at my house that night with all of his stuff." Ruse thought about finding work in California, and of seeing the country. It didn't take him long to make a decision. Having no other plans for the evening, an hour later he found himself climbing into an open freight car.

Across the boxcar sat a couple of seasoned hobos who watched the two clean-cut boys climb into the car. They didn't carry much, and therefore had little to lose, but did think to stuff what little money that they had between their toes down in their shoes. "I was worried if they knew we had it, we'd get clubbed over the head for it. We didn't have much, but in those days, anything was a lot," said Ruse.

Headed west, the train would stop on the fringes of the towns that dotted the landscape. When hunger required it of them, the stowaways might get off of the train as it slowed near the towns and their stations to look for something to eat. With any luck, they might find an overpass with a pot of hot beans roasting over a fire. A few cents could purchase a bowl at "the beanery" and a full stomach along the way.

The Atchison, Topeka, and Santa Fe Railroad took them west, but only in a general sense. The tracks followed the landscape as if they had been put there by gravity itself. The rail would wind its way to the bigger cities and then followed the highways around the little towns along the way; south, west, southwest, south again.

The locomotive made its way south toward Amarillo, then cut down to Canyon, and somewhere along the way, the tracks underneath them decided to turn on out west. The train glanced passed the eight or nine blocks of streets that make up the City of Farwell, Texas and passed into eastern New Mexico, heading over towards Albuquerque. From there, it rolled through the dry prairies toward mountain horizons while the tracks followed alongside a new Highway that had been designated only four years earlier as *U.S. Route 66*.

We Volunteered.

Sitting back against the wall and looking out the door, the landscape appeared motionless, as if the train were hardly moving past the plains and grayish plateaus on the horizon, only speeding up when it passed through a little town whose houses and buildings gave their movements a sense of context, and then disappeared just as quickly as they had come into view.   The landscape was a postcard framed by the door that scrolled past in slow epochs as tranquil as a cloud in the sky.   Only when Ruse dozed off and looked up again would he see the progress the world had made while absent from it.

When the urge struck them, the boys would get off of the train at one of the little towns for a look around. After days of traveling, they hopped from the train at the edge of a small town along the way, hoping to find something to eat. Walking along the tracks into town, a local sheriff stopped the boys and gave them a quiz about where they were headed. "He picked us up and took us to the jail for the night," said Ruse. "We were worried at first, but as it turns out, he just didn't want us getting into trouble sleeping alongside the train tracks that night. Anyway, sleeping in that jail sure was more comfortable than out on the ground or in a box car." The next morning, the sheriff took the boys out to the edge of town to wait for the next train to come.

Hopping the next train, the Santa Fe took them over the desert of Eastern Arizona with its rusty mountains on the horizon and then carried them through the pine forests around Flagstaff and headed southwest, crossing into California below the southern tip of Nevada.

In his young life, Ruse had been on the move many times before, but this travel was different; it was as if the train itself had carried him from one stage of life to another.

II

The California Pine Box Company had been established in 1897 by Erastus James Stanton who was a successful and well-known lumber dealer on the west coast that maintained warehouses all over California. Perhaps true to the frugal culture of his era, Stanton had found that selling uniform pine boxes to crate the fruit from the west coast's bountiful farms and orchards had proven to be as good of a way as any to turn a profit on excess and inferior grade native sugar and white pine from Stanton's lumber business.[1]

For several years, Ruse made his occupation out of a pattern of following seasonal work up to Washington and Oregon driving a tractor and working as a fruit harvester. In the off-season, he would make his way back down to California to work in and out of the mill making and delivering pine boxes. It was this sort of seasonal and yet dependable work that Ruse found himself doing when the first grumblings of World War II broke out.

Warehouse Crew at the California Pine Box Company

We Volunteered.

Carl Ruse on an Oliver Superior Grain Drill.

We Volunteered.

II

In May of 1941, Ruse was spending some time at his father's house in Troup, Texas when he made the decision to enlist in the Army Air Corps. He made the nineteen-mile drive from Troup to Tyler and signed up. Reporting for duty on May 7th, he was immediately sent to March Field California at Riverside. Ruse quickly fell into the routines that the army offered him and enjoyed the camaraderie with the other enlisted men in training there.

His wife to be, Sara, and her family, lived just across the road from his father on their farm in Troup, Texas and he would write back to them regularly from March Field in California. It was September 3rd of 1941 when Ruse penned the following letter to the Tomme family back at home.

Dear Coat and Folks,

Will answer your letter now that I have time. These nights are getting uncomfortably cold and I am sitting here shivering. I sure dread winter. It rains a lot here in the winter time. I doubt if I am here this winter though. I am still thinking of those yellow fever shots. I know of no place in the U.S. where yellow fever is prevalent. Time will go by us as fast in one place as in another. An hour is still sixty seconds long even in Panama, Hawaii, or South America.

I cant get used to $21 per month. I guess I could ask for a raise without fear of getting fired. This is the first job I have ever had where I don't have to worry about getting fired.

I sure was sick last week. I was afraid for a while that I was going to die, then I got worse and I was afraid I wasn't going to die.

I spent the weekend in San Bernardino with some friends. I awoke, looked at my watch and it was 5:15. I jumped out of bed, ran out the back door, and was well on my way to the shower when I realized where I was. I sure was glad all the neighbors were still asleep. I guess I looked foolish out their in my pajamas.

We don't get up until 5:00 (AM) on week days. On Sundays we can sleep as late as we wish. My trouble is that I keep forgetting and get up at the usual time on Sunday. I woke about thirty guys up on Sunday morning before I realized it was Sunday. The following Sunday I woke up and I was tied to the bed.

We have a lot of fun here. It wasn't very funny the other day though. I was boxing with one of the boys. I swung and he ducked, He swung and I ducked, I swung and he ducked, He swung and I forgot to duck. Result – 1 black eye.

We Volunteered.

I am going to get a 3-day pass next week and go to the Grand Canyon. I have a friend in San Bernardino who drives a truck up there every week. He wants me to go along with him.

There was a lot of excitement in the arp Press last week. It seems that some local boy was kidnapped by a kid with a cap pistol. It sure was exciting. I was on pins and needles all the way through.

We always have a little excitement around here. Last week two planes locked wings in mid air and crashed, killing all four occupants. The pilots were both Lieutenants. One was supposed to get married the next day. The girl he was going to marry had already flown out here from San Antonio.

Well, I am going to take a shower. Don't wait so long to write.

Regards,

Carl Ruse

Despite the freedoms and stability that time in the Air Corps was offering thus far, after basic training, life at March Field had become lackluster and monotonous for the young men who wanted to take control of their destination and be nearer to the action, and maybe to see a little of the world. "Things were pretty dull around March Field. We were supposed to go to school to learn something about an airplane, but nothing was going on. So, since we weren't doing anything around there some of us decided we'd rather get out of there," said Ruse. "One day we found a note on our squadron bulletin board calling for volunteers to go to South America, and James Bartlett, a friend of mine who had lived in Santa Anna Texas, decided since we weren't doing anything, we volunteered to go to South America."

Ruse soon learned of his new assignment; the 21st Pursuit Squadron. The 21st was a group of pilots training to fly P-40s. The new volunteers would serve as ground crew for the pilots. "Not long after that those who had volunteered were put on trains and we ended up at Hamilton Field in California, up by San Francisco," said Ruse. "We learned there that our Squadron was getting ready to go overseas. We spent the next two weeks taking shots and doing all the necessary things you need to do prior to going overseas."

Carl Ruse at the California Pine Box Company.

We Volunteered.

CHAPTER II

NOT IN SOUTH AMERICA

A Japanese attack on Pearl Harbor is a Strategic Impossibility.

George Fielding Eliot
September 1938

It was a Saturday night, November 1st, 1941 when the 21st Pursuit Squadron's Commander, twenty-five-year-old Ed Dyess, along with thirteen pilots and their ground crew set sail from San Francisco.[1] Ruse, a new recruit, remembers shipping out with destination unknown: "Finally we boarded a ship, the *President Coolidge* which was a luxury liner before they turned it into a troop ship. Thinking we were going to South America we left under the Golden Gate Bridge. Several days later when we arrived at Honolulu, we knew doggone well that we weren't going to South America."

Only after arriving in Manila, did the men of the 21st deduce that "PLUM", the codeword for their new assignment, meant Philippines, Luzon, Manila, and thus, their destination was certainly not South America. Yet, the trip across the Pacific on the old luxury liner was a pleasant one. While it had been converted to a troop ship, the *President Coolidge* retained some of the amenities of a luxury liner. The men ate fine meals cafeteria style in the ship's dining hall, where waiters did much of the serving.[2] The ship was still outfitted with two swimming pools, a gym, a sun deck, and a theater where movies were watched every night.[3] Dyess described passing the trip as one occupied with "a few drinks, song fests, poker games, swimming, boxing bouts, deck games, lectures, bull sessions, and picture shows."[4]

While the *Coolidge* cruised, American relations with Japan continued to decline (as they had since the end of the Grant administration), and with hostile acts committed by Japan increasing in recent months, tensions between the two nations only grew.[5] In July of that year, Japan had invaded southern Indochina and seized air and naval bases, positioning it for strikes of the Dutch East Indies and Malaya. This perceived threat to peace lead to retaliation by freezing of Japanese assets on the order of President Franklin Delano Roosevelt on July 26th.

At the same time, the U.S. government began to reorganize American and Filipino defensive forces in the Philippines by forming a single operational command – the United States Army Forces in the Far East (USAFFE). General Douglas MacArthur was called to service to serve as Major General and Commander of the USAFFE forces.[6] Previously, President Roosevelt had been consumed with the war in Europe, and consequentially, the situation in the Pacific was receiving less attention. Discussions with Japan had been handled by the state department, with no particular sense of urgency.[7]

In August, MacArthur learned that the 200th Coast Artillery Regiment and the 194th Tank Battalion were being assigned to his command. He would also be shipped fifty new P-40E pursuit planes. A month later, in a memo to MacArthur, General H.B. Clagett outlined the needs of the forces in order to effectively operate the newly formed force. His analysis showed a need for twenty-seven squadrons of pursuit aircraft, thirty squadrons of heavy bombers, and eighteen squadrons of light bombers, based on the assumption that the Japanese had an extensive force on Formosa for the purpose of attacking the Philippines.

A lack of suitable airfields would slow any such expansion. For such growth, fifty-six would be needed, while ten existed at the time. Growth of this newly designated Far East Air Force (FEAF) would have to happen fast. MacArthur was given priority of all new B-17s as they came off of production lines, and was scheduled to have a total of two-hundred and forty P-40Es by December 31st.

On their way across the Pacific, the *Coolidge* made a brief stop in Honolulu, arriving in the early morning hours of November 5th. Sailing into Pearl Harbor at Dawn with a view of Diamond's Head at sunrise, the men were given nine hours to spend on shore before setting sail again in the afternoon. They made the most of the stop by taking in Waikiki Beach and the Royal Hawaiian Hotel.

The Squadron left Oahu, and moved on toward the Philippines, relieved that the war had not arrived there before they had, having heard news all along the way about mounting hostilities with the Japanese. The ship joined a convoy as it traveled past Guam, picking up another troop transporter, the *Hugh L. Scott*, and the *Astoria* to serve as an armed naval escort as it headed into potentially hostile waters.[8]

Commander Ed Dyess later said "For weeks we had all been convinced that war with Japan was imminent."[9] This added to a sense of urgency and intensity to the Squadron's transport of pilots and crew. Ruse recalls this intensity in the passage from Honolulu on to Manila for the rest of the trip after November 6th; "We had blackouts every night, and we weren't allowed to smoke on deck," said Ruse. In the passageways of the ship, port-holes were sealed and tiny blue lights provided only just enough light for the men to avoid collisions while moving through the crowded ship. Fire and life-boat drills were done routinely, with a degree of slow-moving chaos as so many men blocked doors and passageways leading to the deck.

II

On November 20th, the *Coolidge* dropped anchor in waters just off of Guam. The ship was too large to enter the shallow channel that entered the ports, so only the two convoy ships docked on the Island. Providing further evidence of their nearing some action, the Cruiser that was traveling in convoy with the *Coolidge* catapulted four airplanes into the air to stand guard while the *Scott* and the *Astoria* docked. Some of the men on deck took advantage of the brief stop to do some fishing while others swam and exercised in the gym. The ship was underway again by 1:00PM.

As the *President Coolidge* crossed the International Date Line in the Pacific, tensions between Washington and Tokyo grew, as evidenced by strained diplomatic efforts between the two capitals. "We arrived at Manila on November the 20th, 1941," said Ruse.

USS *President Coolidge*

The 21st Pursuit Squadron disembarked at 9:00 A.M. from *The President Coolidge* at Pier Seven in the South Harbor of Manila, while the sounds of a Filipino band playing "Dixie" welcomed them onto the docks. The men were greeted by a group of soldiers and civilians, and then loaded onto Army trucks and headed to their new home; Nichols Field.

The trucks moved from the port area through the city and onto Taft Avenue, and then through the suburb of Pasay. They then drove through the village of Baclaran where they turned left across a narrow stream of murky water, and onto the perimeter of Nichols Field.

The base was not much more than a cluster of buildings and a few hangars just beyond the bridge from Baclaran, as well as a handful of barracks, concession shops, an un-air-conditioned movie theater (really a shed with chicken-wire walls), a small library, and the Post-Exchange which included a popular restaurant and beer garden. All of the bases' few buildings were on two roads that formed a letter "T". There was a softball field and a nine-hole golf course with a small hamburger joint next to it that was known as *the tenth hole*. The barracks were simple buildings with low-overhanging eaves and a low-angled roof and latticed windows that remained open except for during a storm.[10]

About one hundred yards from the barracks was a detached mess hall that was staffed by cheap Filipino labor which was paid for by a small fee from the pay of all privates and corporals. The men were served family-style, with food brought to the tables. Two other fees were deducted from paychecks at Nichols – one for barracks cleaning and one for laundry service.[11]

In times leading up to the war, life at Nichols was leisurely for the men working there, but by the time the men of the 21st Pursuit arrived at the field things had changed. They were just in time to miss out on the easygoing atmosphere that residents of the base had previously known.

The men were set hastily to work in preparing for a possible Japanese invasion and for life in the Philippines. They had arrived to an atmosphere in which imminent war was expected, and Manila was a likely first target. "The first thing we did at Nichols Field was to listen to a Doctor brief us on the Philippines," said Ruse. "He warned us not to eat any of the native food there, and by all means *never* to eat in any of the cafes there in downtown Manila, but to eat out of our own Squadron mess. I often wondered after that how we made it through the things that we had to go through later on, had we not eaten native food, and things that were really worse than native food."

The Squadron had been shipped out in a hurry, without any airplanes; however, new planes (still in their shipping crates) were to be delivered for them soon after their arrival at Nichols Field. On November 26th, any possible delay of war with Japan seemed even less of a possibility when diplomatic efforts broke down as Japan refused to cease hostilities in China and elsewhere. Just two weeks prior to the attack on Pearl Harbor, the ground crews of the 21st were just getting started with the process of assembling their airplanes. "We arrived two weeks before the Japs hit Pearl Harbor, and we were in the process of getting our planes ready for flight. We had them all out in a field behind the Post Exchange at Nichols Field," said Ruse.

Since they had little time to prepare, the state of affairs at Nichols was primitive; however the operating conditions for pilots had just recently been improved. The simple airfield had been notorious for its tendency for flooding and marshy terrain, often submerging the runways during the rainy seasons, and had been under construction during much of 1941. The east-west runway had been paved and extended, as it had previously only been useable during the dry season. The north-south runway was improved by filling in low-lying areas, and a new northeast-southwest runway had been graded.[12]

Four days after their arrival at Nichols, the 21st were first issued some worn P-35s. The first of the new and yet unassembled P-40s were not even ready for use until November 28th, only days before Pearl Harbor was attacked, and the still-in-crates airplanes did not even arrive in the Philippines until November 25th.[13] By December 8th, a total of twenty-two planes were operational.[a] Around each of the planes, the squadron's Armorers had stacked wooden boxes of .50-caliber ammunition, and the filthy job of boiling the thick, waxy, rust-preventative, cosmoline off of the guns following their removal of the crates was done so that the guns could be mounted onto the planes and boresighted.

The best was made of the resources available. Ruse remembered their surroundings upon arrival: "Since there was no

---

[a] This number is from a 1943 interview of Ed Dyess by Priestly (Ed Dyess, interview by William Priestley, Cabanatuan POW Camp, 1943, Priestley Papers)

hangar space available for us, it became necessary to assemble our ships right out in the open. We had them spaced out about a hundred feet apart directly behind the Nichols Field Post Exchange. There was a softball diamond, and we were out there working on the planes and were getting them ready for flight. Most of our planes were still in crates at this time." The ground crews at Nichols were working twenty-four hours a day just to assemble the new airplanes, and a long and heavy runway was still being built by civilians in order to adequately accommodate the heavy B-17s.[14]

Maj. Gen. Lewis Brereton, a new commanding General, had stopped to inspect Nichols Field during the week of November 10th-15th. As he entered the air depot's hangar, he described what he saw as "completely inadequate." He found zero spare parts for any of the P-40s being assembled. Additionally, the depot had very few tools available to make "even rudimentary repair and maintenance." As a consequence, the Nichols Field Air Depot was put on a two-shift, sixteen hour workday.[15]

On November 28th, news reached USAFFE that ongoing diplomatic negotiations had broken down with Japan. It seemed that some sort of hostilities with Japan were inevitable. In the first days of December, all personnel at Nichols were ordered to wear their steel "doughboy" helmets, and be equipped with gas masks at all times. Seven machine gun placements were being built and fortified all around the airfield.[16]

Midmorning on December 6th, far-eastern time, Commander Dyess was summoned to Headquarters by Brigadier General Harold H. George. General George got to the point. "He looked at us in somber silence as we walked into the long room and sat down on benches and chairs." Then General George spoke: "Men, you are not a suicide squadron yet, but you're damned close to it. There will be war with Japan in a few days. It may come in a few hours." Just outside that building, the motors of the new P-40s were audible as they were still on testing blocks. General George continued: "The Japs have a minimum of three-thousand planes they can send down from Formosa and from aircraft carriers. They know the way already. When they come again, they will be tossing something." General George went on to give the Squadron Commanders an estimate of the number of planes that would be needed to defend the islands against the Japanese (five to eight groups), and they all knew that the resources were simply not there yet. General George bluntly concluded: "Well, that's the job you will be facing within a very short time."[17]

For several days already, Japanese planes had been flying over Luzon and some of the other Philippine islands. At 2:30 A.M. on December 8th, the Squadron was ordered to stations for the sixth successive day. None of the eighteen planes on the field had been in the air more than three hours. Meanwhile, at a Manila Hotel, MacArthur was awakened from his sleep at 3:55 A.M. Manila time, and was informed that Pearl Harbor had been attacked at 2:35 A.M.

That morning the telephone rang and Commander Dyess told the men that the Japanese had "taken the plunge", but had bypassed the Philippines for the time being, and had bombed Pearl Harbor to their east. As pilots hurriedly dressed and headed for the airfield, some thought it was a false alarm. 2nd Lt. Dave Olbert thought upon hearing that Pearl Harbor was attacked "It's just another rumor. How could Japanese bombers reach Hawaii?" Available pilots moved their planes to the east end of the runway and shut down the engines to await orders over the radio; many of them were not yet in uniform. The pilots of the 21st had been awakened at 2:30 A.M., being told that there was an emergency, but still unaware that Pearl Harbor had been bombed. Ten minutes later, the pilots went back to their quarters, only to be awakened again two hours later with the unfathomable news that Pearl Harbor had been attacked.[18] Ruse remembers the day as one spent digging, and later occupying a fox-hole: "My introduction to the fox-hole came on the 8th of December while we were working on those planes," he said.

Finally, confirmation came that Pearl Harbor had in fact been attacked. Work on preparing additional planes finally had to be ceased so that ground crews could prepare for attack: "We got word that the Japs had bombed Pearl Harbor, and knew that we would probably be next in line for a visit from the Japs, so that morning found us busily engaged in digging foxholes right on the softball diamond around the planes we were working on so we'd have a place to get into in case of an air raid," said Ruse.

While Nichols was a likely target, it was uncertain as to who might be struck first. There were other airfields such as nearby Clark Field that were probable targets as well. After waiting on alert with their planes all morning, the pilots of the 21st Pursuit Squadron were called to the operations tent by Dyess where a tub of Coca-Cola, sandwiches, and olives were waiting for them. At 11:45, a phone rang and Dyess answered. Orders had come over the radio to Nichols base: "Tally-ho, Clark field!" [19]

The men ran for their planes, and Dyess took off immediately, with the other fifteen planes following him up. Another flight left fifteen minutes later; its crew had just finishing the assembly of a new P-40. They climbed to 24,000 feet and were off to Clark Field, forty miles north of Nichols. After taking off, the pilots were ordered to change course to intercept Japanese bombers, but their small force was unable to stop the bombing.

On the ground at Clark Field, the Japanese planes came into sight of those on the ground. Sgt. Bill King of the 20th Pursuit fired his pistol into the air three times as a warning of an air raid, then got on the phone to inform group operations. Fifty-four planes had been counted in V formations, now almost directly overhead. When the phone was answered by First Lt. Benny Putnam, the Commanding Officer of the Headquarters Squadron, King said to sound the air raid alarm because Japanese planes were approaching. Major Grover, upon hearing the message said; "How does he know they are Japanese planes?" King then yelled to Putnam, "We don't have so Goddamn many!" Within seconds, bombs were falling directly over their heads. The men sounded the air-raid and ran for a trench. [20]

Another pilot in the 21st, Sam Grashio, had just taken off, but had become separated from Dyess and made his way to Clark where the field was already burning and heavy fighting was taking place. He arrived back at Nichols in a shot-up P-40. After exiting the plane at Nichols he said to Dyess: "By God, They ain't shootin' spitballs are they?" The right aileron of his P-40 had been nearly shot off, and there was a hole in the wing so big "you could throw a hat through." [21] At Clark Field, only eight hours after the attack on Pearl Harbor, the Japanese had found half of the U.S. Far East Air Force lined up, wing to wing on an unprotected field. [22]

We Volunteered.

Nichols Field in 1941

III

As Clark Field was being heavily attacked only forty miles away, the ground crews at Nichols Field were busily digging foxholes, and preparing for attack. With all of the airplanes available for their defense already in the air, there was little else that could be done to defend themselves. Finally, as some of the Squadron's planes returned and were being serviced after their morning outing, the Japanese bombers made their way to Nichols Field.

By this time, there was very little that the men at Nichols field could do to defend themselves other than to keep on digging and get themselves underground. "I was one of a group working under a Sergeant Dort, an old Staff Sergeant in our outfit," said Ruse. "The crew I was working in decided we would dig a foxhole out on the pitcher's mound of the softball diamond. We had just begun to dig when, luckily for us, Dort came by and said, 'I don't believe it's wise to put it there.' He said, 'Why not put it over at third base, that way it will be half way between those planes over there and the crews from both planes can get in there in case of an air-raid.'" The men took Sergeant Dort's advice and began working on a new foxhole near third-base.

At the time Ruse would have no idea of how, in the months ahead, the fox-hole would become a very familiar place for him. "If all the fox-holes (and latrines) that I dug during my time in the Philippines were laid end to end, I believe they would reach from Manila to San Francisco. It is surprising how one, although both physically and mentally exhausted can still find the strength to dig another foxhole," he said.

At 11:30 A.M. Ruse had just finished his fox-hole and was filling sand-bags to place around the top when he heard the low-rumbling sound of aircraft engines in the distance. "In a matter of seconds, we saw what we thought was one of ours coming in. Since there were a few planes at Nichols, we figured one of them was coming in for a landing. The plane appeared to be a P-36 coming in low over one of the landing strips, but when we looked up and saw the red balls of the rising sun insignia on the wings and fuselage, and heard the firing machine-gun chatter, this assumption was quickly proven incorrect, so in a fraction of a second, the fox-hole we had just made had its first and last tenants. It was the first time we'd ever used a bomb shelter, so we got in it in a hurry," said Ruse.

All the men could do was keep low and watch as the strafing of their airfield dragged on. The anti-aircraft fire that chattered around the corners of the field did little to deter the strafing Japanese fighter pilots. "These Jap zeroes, as the planes proved to be, strafed our field there and strafed us for probably an hour, and then we could hear the two-motored heavy bombers coming down the flight-line," said Ruse.

As the bombs would fall, there would be no sound, but suddenly there would be a deafening blast immediately followed by a violent concussion that emanated out in a thudding shockwave.

As they lay low in the trench, the bombs were in fact falling nearer and nearer as the bombers flew down the length of the flight-line. "We were unable to hear the bombs falling, but could hear them hit and feel the concussion," said Ruse. "They were dropping bombs and it seemed like each bomb kept coming closer and closer and closer, when suddenly there was a deafening roar and everything was obliterated from view. A bomb had hit close enough that it threw dirt in on all over us, and about that time I thought another one would land right in our hole. We gave a big sigh of release when the next bomb hit the Post Exchange and we knew that the bombers had banked to the left," said Ruse.

Lying low in the foxhole, Ruse heard a scream next to him; "Someone yelled 'Gas!', so I started feeling for my gas mask but, much to my consternation, my mask had disappeared. By this time, I was the only occupant of the hole who didn't have a gas mask on, but it suddenly dawned on me that the fellow who had yelled 'Gas' had probably smelled the burned powder from the bomb that had fallen so close to us and I felt greatly relieved."

"After the raid (which had lasted about two and one-half hours) was all over with, we climbed out of the hole to survey what was left of Nichols Field," said Ruse. "The first object to catch my eye was my gas mask over near a sand bag I had been filling."

Then we all saw a huge crater in the dead center of that pitcher's mound. It was right where we had started to dig that fox-hole, and we were really glad we hadn't built it on the pitcher's mound! I guess we were very lucky that we didn't. Dort's decision to dig on third base instead of the pitcher's mound saved us from a direct hit by a five hundred pound bomb. I learned early that a little hole in the ground could sometimes be the difference between life and death."

We Volunteered.

Nichols Field under attack on December 10th, 1941. (Morton 1953)

IV

At the end of the day, the 17th and the 21st were the only fully-equipped Pursuit Squadrons left to defend the Philippines; but with the airstrip at Nichols destroyed, at present time, they did not have a home to fly out of. The FEAF had taken a crucial blow on December 8th. At Clark field, of a force of thirty-five B-17s, half were now reduced to wreckage, along with nearly twenty P-40s. North of Manila at Iba, the sole operational radar station had been destroyed, blinding USAFFE of the ability to see coming attacks in the future Seven P-40s caught on the field were also destroyed. Six others had been shot down or damaged beyond repair. Of ninety-two P-40s that were flyable at the beginning of the tack, now only fifty-eight remained in flyable condition.[23] The Japanese also demolished the sole operational radar set,. The Japanese lost only seven fighters in the attacks.[24]

As men at Nichols attempted to rest after the attacks, they were awakened once by a false-alarm, and then a second alarm at 3:15 A.M. on December 9th. This time, the Japanese Naval Air Force was in the area. Seven twin-engine "Nell" bombers began unloading on the base once again. Fortunately, on December 9th, a heavy fog over the Formosan Islands had forced the Japanese to cancel plans for the day. By the next day, news came to MacArthur that the Japanese had made small landings on Northern Luzon, Aparri, and Vigan.

Orders came now for the immediate abandonment of Nichols Field. With its position well-known to the Japanese, and few resources to defend it, the men there would have to find another airfield to call home. "Everything we had at Nichols field was destroyed, so there was no further reason for us to continue our stay there," said Ruse. "All of our planes that weren't in the shape to go up yet had been destroyed on the ground. Lieutenant Ball, Our Squadron Adjutant sent us word to meet at a certain spot in a grove of trees near the field. We met at the designated time and we were ordered to walk into the outskirts of Manila just off of the famed Dewey Boulevard."[b]

---

[b] Dewey Boulevard is presently referred to as Roxas Boulevard.

We Volunteered.

By 5:30 P.M., the remaining planes at Nichols were sent to Clark Field in hopes that they would avoid subsequent, more severe attacks on Nichols Field.[25] This proved to be the best decision. Between 12:45 and 1:00 P.M. on December 10th, two attack groups consisting of fifty-two Zeros and eighty-one "Betty" and "Nell" bombers returned to the area to wipe out Nichols and Del Carmen Fields as well as the Cavite Navy Yard, just south of Manila. By December 12th, MacArthur's FEAF had been reduced to a point where he was forced to conserve his P-40s for reconnaissance only, saying: "Pilots have been ordered to avoid direct combat." MacArthur would soon have greater threats to manage: In the early morning of December 22nd, a force of over forty three thousand Japanese troops landed in Lingayen Gulf from some eighty transports, and in subsequent days made rapid advances down Luzon with little resistance. Ironically, this was the same date that MacArthur was promoted to four-star rank as a General.[26]

Meanwhile, Japanese attacks were happening at a frenzied pace, with attacks occurring in Hawaii, Guam, Wake, Borneo, Java, Malaya, Singapore, Hong Kong, and several places in the Philippines concurrently.[27] It had not even been two months since Ruse and the men of the 21st Pursuit Squadron set sail past the Golden Gate Bridge and into the Pacific.

CHAPTER III

MANILA

In order to spare the metropolitan area from possible ravages of attack either by air or ground, Manila is hereby declared an open city without the characteristics of a military objective. In order that no excuse may be given for a possible mistake, the American High Commissioner, the Commonwealth government, and all combatant military installations will be withdrawn from its environs as rapidly as possible.

General Douglas MacArthur
December 27, 1941

Manila was a beautiful city. Although it was thousands of miles from San Francisco, many soldiers had become quite comfortable there in months and years leading up to the war, having found a pleasant and comfortable place to pass their time in the service. Of course, that outlook came to an abrupt end by December 9th of 1941.

Ruse packed his few things and headed for the city, following orders to abandon the destroyed Nichols field. "We were a sad and dejected group on that march into Manila. Several of our buddies, victims of the Japanese bombs and bullets, were left behind. We were able to salvage very few of our personal belongings and many of the boys did not know how to use the Springfield Rifles issued to us before leaving Nichols," said Ruse.

We Volunteered.

There was no headquarters or appropriate facilities in Manila, so the men were instructed to pair up and stay nearby each other in a residential area near Dewey Boulevard. They were to attempt to find places to sleep bedded down wherever they could find. "We found a place we could spend the night bedded down in someone's back yard in the adjoining neighborhood," said Ruse.

Meanwhile, Lieutenant Ball set up a Squadron Adjutant's headquarters in the neighborhood where the men camped, and instructed the men to come there to retrieve canned daily rations. "We all just scattered out around an area close to a church that was in the vicinity. We were to keep in contact with Lieutenant Ball until we received orders from our Squadron Commander, Captain Dyess, who had been up at Clark Field when the raid on Nichols took place," said Ruse.

"Lieutenant Ball appointed several boys to serve as runners and the balance of us split off into small groups. When each group found a place to stay, we were to notify headquarters so that a runner could find them if and when they were needed," said Ruse. "I sought out my buddy, a friend of mine in our outfit, Wendell Bates from California. He and I got together and went over there to Manila in search of a place to stay. We found a nice looking home there that had a nice back yard with a rock wall around it. Without asking permission, we climbed over the fence, made ourselves at home, and prepared to spend the night."

"Our first night in Manila pretty well steeled both Bates and myself for the days to come," said Ruse. "We were cognizant of our immediate surroundings since our first move upon arrival in our new location was to learn the lay of the land. Knowing that no lights would be allowed in the city, we decided that it would be a very good idea to become acquainted with the terrain. Bates and I had just settled down anticipating a few hours shut eye when at about midnight we heard a voice from just over the wall on Dewey Boulevard say, "Turn those damned lights off!" After what seemed to us like an interminable silence, this order was repeated and was followed immediately by what sounded like shots from a forty-five caliber automatic."

"Since I was never the nosey type when trouble seemed imminent, I was for going to sleep and forgetting the whole episode, but Old Bates wasn't buying any of this, and being a very curious type of person decided to go look and see what was going on, so I soon found myself following him over the wall toward Dewey Boulevard."

"After stumbling through the darkness for about five minutes we heard a voice say, "I'm sorry, sir. Orders are orders and my orders are to put out all lights and if necessary, I am to use force in carrying out my assignment. After turning in the direction from whence the sounds had come, we soon found their source. We found a Corporal in the MP's with a forty-five automatic in his hand talking to a Naval Lieutenant. They were standing beside an automobile with the letters "U.S.N." on it signifying that it belonged to the United States Navy."

"The Lieutenant was very indignant. It seemed that he disliked the idea of having to take orders from a mere Corporal, but after being reminded that a war was going on, he continued on his way minus his headlights," said Ruse.

"I have heard the old saying, 'Curiosity killed the cat.' I don't know how true it is, but I do know that curiosity deprived me of any sleep that first night in Manila. I am referring to the curiosity of a certain character named Bates. After the episode with the Naval Lieutenant, Bates said 'This looks like fun, lets help 'em.' So we spent the rest of the night with the Navy over there on Dewey Boulevard. He may or may not have been a descendant of one of the old lamp-lighters of early days, but I honestly believe that one of his ancestors must have delighted in extinguishing lamps since Bates spent the remainder of the night putting out lights," said Ruse.

"Several broken lights and neon signs later dawn came and we decided that it might be a good idea to report to headquarters. Upon arrival at headquarters, we learned that our status had not changed during the night and that we were still awaiting orders. After picking up a few cans of rations from a supply on hand at headquarters, we started back to the place where we had intended to spend the previous night. We were passing one of the nicer looking homes in the vicinity when we passed the house where we spent the night in the back yard. A young Filipino Fellow of about seventeen came to the door and asked us in and said his family would like for us to come into their home and eat with them at mealtime. I looked at Bates and said, 'Why not?'"

"We entered a modern well-furnished living room and saw an elderly Filipino couple and two more young fellows, one appearing to be about twenty, and the other twenty-two. After introductions, we were told that we had been seen wandering about the streets and that these people would be happy to furnish us a place to sleep. We accepted their hospitality and, knowing that food had already become scarce, we turned in our sea-rations to them. Our first meal with these friendly people was one I will never forget. They had a wonderful cook (it was a well-to-do family who had a cook), who prepared our canned sea rations in such a manner that even we could hardly recognize them. During the entire meal a servant girl fanned us with a palm leaf. One look at Bates convinced me that he had found something he liked even better than putting out lights."

"Our stay in the back-yard with our newly-found host lasted for about two days, and on about the third day the stay was abruptly terminated. One of the runners came and told us one night that we were to report to headquarters. We would be moving out and were going up to a field, a cane patch, up toward Bataan where they had prepared a landing field for us," said Ruse.

II

After arriving at headquarters, the men learned that their orders had come through and that they were expected to move out that night. The men all loaded into a few old buses and headed out. "Our next stop was Santo Tomas University where we spent the balance of the night and the following day," said Ruse.

"During our stay at Santo Tomas we were able to get a little firsthand information on how the war was progressing from a Captain who had just returned from the northern end of the island," said Ruse. "I learned that the Japs had made two landings in force; one at Aparri and the other at Lingayen Gulf. Since the American Forces in the Philippines had had no time to prepare for an invasion at those points they were steadily being pushed back on all fronts. The future looked very dark indeed for our side; particularly since the Japs had boasted that they would be in Manila by Christmas. From all indications this boast was well on its way to becoming a reality," said Ruse. "Little did we know as we left Manila that night by bus, the next time we would see the city, all of its beautiful buildings would be reduced to a mass of rubble."

Presently, large black plumes of smoke rose to the sky and out over the bay from the Navy storage area between Nichols Field and Cavite, a little claw of land that reached out into the Manila bay. One million gallons of oil were being burned so that it did not have to be left in the hands of the Japanese.[1] The destruction of Manila was far from being over.

PHILIPPINE SEA

SOUTH
CHINA
SEA

APARRI

VIGAN

LINGAYEN
GULF

● BAGUIO

● ROSALES

● TARLAC
● CLARK

LUZON

IBA ●

● LUBAO

MANILA
● NIELSON
BATAAN ● NICHOLS
CAVITE

CORREGIDOR

MINDORO

SIBUYAN SEA

N
W ⊕ E
S

VISAYAN SEA

MASBATE

CHAPER IV

THE AIR STRIP AT LUBAO

On the road ahead there lies hard work -- grueling work --
day and night, every hour and every minute.

Franklin Delano Roosevelt
Fireside Chat
December 9th, 1941

The pilots of the 21st had done everything possible to defend Nichols and Clark Field, but running out of resources and with their enemy approaching, the Squadron was re-organized, and would need to move out immediately to a new airfield. A line of old buses and G.I. trucks arrived to transport the men to the new airfield. Ruse climbed into a bus and settled in for bumpy ride. "The old buses and G.I. trucks had Filipino drivers, and they were the wildest drivers I ever rode with. Our driver, a Filipino who must have been one of those wild cab drivers in prewar Manila, slowed down for nothing. We had no lights that night, since we were having blackout. How he knew where he was going in the darkness will always be a mystery to me. In spite of our apprehensions, we arrived safely at our destination shortly before dawn the next morning. I did not know then that I was in for some rougher ones later as "Guest" of the Japanese after the fall of Bataan," said Ruse.

We Volunteered.

The new airfield was near Lubao, about fifty miles northwest of Manila in Pampanga province. It had been picked out by General George himself during a search of the area for new airfield sites, in an attempt to stay ahead of the advancing forces.

Ruse arrived at this new and secret airstrip on the evening of December 15th: "When we finally stopped before daylight the next morning we were in this open cane-patch." Lubao field was supposed to have already been completed, however, upon first inspection by Dyess, the runway was still under construction, and revetments within which to conceal the planes still had not been constructed. "We had heard several rumors that we were going to get airplanes and supplies from Australia and now we found ourselves preparing to build an airfield for these rumored planes. Approximately two hundred Filipino Laborers had already been working to make the selected spot suitable for an airfield before we had arrived."

Given the urgent need for an airstrip, Dyess set the laborers and men of the 21st to work in shifts twenty-four hours a day, along with the 71st Engineering Battalion (Philippine Army).[1] The enlisted men of the 21st set immediately to work building and camouflaging the new airfield.

Attired in old denims and straw hats, the enlisted men set to work cutting cane and digging revetments for planes along with the local laborers. Ruse "With their help, we began by cutting the cane out through the center of the field in a swath about one hundred feet wide through the center of the field. The strip was to serve as the runway and from the air it appeared only to be a cane patch in which the cane had been partially cut," said Ruse.

While work was happening twenty-four-seven, exposed work on the surface of the airfield and revetments posed a constant risk of being seen by Japanese reconnaissance planes and bombers. "Since the Jap planes always flew over our cane patch on their way to bomb Manila and Corregidor we had to do all our work at night. Help from Australia, never did actually arrive. Since hangars were out of the question, we had chicken wire strung over the top of the dug-in revetments where they could cut fresh cane every night and stick down into the chicken wire to look like the cane patch was all still there and camouflage the plane. The wire was hung over the

34

revetments at a height level with the surrounding cane. Each night, fresh cane was cut from the back side of the field and tied to the wire so that from the air our revetments would appear to be part of the uncut cane. After we had only been there a couple of days we had our field ready for our expected planes to operate from."

Twelve parking strips had been constructed at a right-angle to the airstrip with the revetments dug in front of each of them sized 40' X 20' to fit the airplanes, and surrounded by sandbags at a depth of five feet. Also in front of each revetment, a line of bamboo cups about two feet in length and two feet apart were placed in the soil, with sugar cane sections placed in them so that their tops matched the height of the live cane growing on the other half of the field. These walls could be quickly pulled out to allow a plane out onto the field.[2]

Life for Ruse and the other enlisted men at Lubao had been tough during the construction period. They built and lived in portable nipa shacks made from bamboo. They sweltered in heat and humidity during the day, and fought mosquitoes by night. Fortunately, however, they had food and other supplies trucked in from Manila. The officers and senior noncoms lived in a house eight miles west of the field in San Benito. The house included a chapel and sixteen rooms. When the Americans moved in, the Filipino family moved to a small building in the compound near the house.[3]

II

Finally on Christmas Eve, twenty-six planes that remained after the initial December 8th attacks arrived. There were twenty-five P-40s and an A-27, which had been used for both attack and dive bombing arrived at Lubao.[4] That evening, MacArthur evacuated with his staff to the fortified island of Corregidor in Manila Bay. On Christmas Day, he received word from the War Department that plans to ferry P-40s from Australia to the Philippines had been "Jeopardized".

We Volunteered.

Japanese planes on a mission over Bataan. National Archives

The Air Strip at Lubao

As the Japanese advance headed southward, the airfields on Borneo in the Dutch East Indies were threatened, hindering the possibility of refueling the short ranged pursuit planes. Resources at Lubao and other airfields would remain sparse.

Dyess describes the first landing at the new airfield at Lubao: "The first plane to come in hit a soft spot on the field, bounded into the air in a complete somersault, and hit on its nose...Three hundred Filipinos ran wildly onto the field like so many chickens." They were directly in the path of the other planes which were just dropping in. It looked as if a mass tragedy was inevitable. The next I remember, I was running at them, yelling like a wild Indian and firing my automatic. The bullets were whining just over their heads. Those boys were off the field and into a cane patch in nothing flat. They didn't come back for hours."[5]

The same day, General Douglas MacArthur was leaving his Manila Headquarters. He was now in the field, fighting an enemy that was quickly advancing. Christmas dinner of 1941 was the Squadron's last large meal for some time. The pilots and enlisted men spent Christmas dinner at a Hacienda about ten miles from Lubao Field. While the Philippine Capital City of Manila had been declared an open city that day, this made it possible to send into the city for anything that was needed. Dyess remembers eating turkey, canned cranberry sauce, plum pudding, vegetables and coffee, and even "a few drops of holiday cheer." [6]

Camouflaging the airfield was an ongoing challenge. The 3,500-foot runway was divided into two halves. One half was covered with dead cane which looked from above as if it had been cut. The other section was left bare, like a newly planted field. The cane was removed and replaced before each takeoff. The bare section of the field was swept of any tire tracks. The field was alongside a road that would be blasted by Japanese fighters and dive bombers regularly, which left the field in danger of being discovered at any time.

On one occasion, a Japanese bomber was flying over the field after hitting a bridge just two miles away. As it flew over, an anti-aircraft gun just across the highway from the field opened up. Dyess remembers looking up and seeing the plane hit: "I could see daylight between the fuselage and the port engine. The next instant, planes burst through the bomb doors and billowed out behind the plane, which keeled over and started down." Not knowing which way the plane would fall, Dyess stood still and watched it turn, coming closer and closer to the earth. "From where I stood, it looked like he would hit me right between the eyes. When the ship was within a hundred feet of the ground, I started hot-footing it." The plane struck into the cane patch and caused a fire, and all hands turned out to extinguish it before others could be attracted to the smoke. The explosion scattered maps and charts and papers over a wide area, which Dyess instructed the laborers to gather up. "They obeyed to the letter, one of them handing me the jawbones and big teeth of a Jap flyer."[7]

Manila is declared an open city by MacArthur. Japanese Photograph (Morton 1953)

III

With no replenishment from the outside, MacArthur's small Far East Air Force was getting smaller and smaller each week. Many planes were lost, either in air combat, or even getting cracked up upon landing in the dusty and sometimes soft ground on Luzon.

Despite their best efforts to conceal it, the airfield at Lubao was soon discovered. Work was finally finished on the airfield on the morning of New Year's Day, 1942. By afternoon, they learned that the Japanese were advancing and the field was considered front line territory. By evening, Ruse and other members of the ground crew learned that orders had been given to abandon it. "We discovered someone started shooting flares around the field at night. Since the same thing had happened to us at Nichols Field, we knew that we could expect Jap planes in the near future. Just as we expected, they came and started working on our airfield immediately with the heavy bombers, concentrating mainly on the runway."

On the night of January 2nd, 1942, Captain Dyess told his men that another move was in store for them. "Boys," said Dyess. "You know what happens when you lose your airplanes?" he inquired. Undoubtedly met with looks of uncertainty, Dyess looked at his men and said; "You're infantry." "Now let's go get the guns cleaned up…cause you're gonna be using them."[8]

"We were going to move out that night and go up into Bataan because the Japs had started bombing where we were, and that they were wise to the fact that we had started building an airfield there," said Ruse. "Captain Dyess had learned that the Japs had occupied the City of San Fernando and could very easily be among us by the following morning if we were still around. This called for another hasty departure since we were not equipped to hold them off."

"After gathering what equipment we could carry and destroying the remainder, we met at an old Filipino Church near the cane field. It was midnight and we were waiting for our transportation when I heard several voices speaking excitedly in Tagalog, one of the native dialects spoken on the island of Luzon.

After investigating we learned that a group of the locals had caught another Filipino shooting flares. I gathered from the gist of their conversation that they were unanimously in favor of relieving him of his head on the spot. He was a wild-eyed looking one, and you could tell he was scared. Having seen them in action with their razor sharp bolos, which is a knife with a blade about twenty inches long that they used for nearly everything they did or built, I for one did not envy their prisoner. After further consultation, they all agreed to leave the matter up to Captain Dyess," said Ruse.

"Our buses were just arriving when the Filipinos told Captain Dyess that he was the one who had been shooting the flares, and they asked what he wanted them to do with the prisoner," said Ruse. As Dyess climbed into one of the busses, he said "You fellows caught him." He said, "He's all yours, boys. You do whatever you want to with him. We are leaving and it's up to you to take care of it," recalled Ruse. "We left immediately and were not on hand to witness the end of the little drama but there has never been a doubt in my mind as to how it ended. We never in any way doubted that he lost his head that night."

IV

As the men of the 21st Pursuit Squadron abandoned the airfield on which they had completed work the very same day, Japanese forces were advancing. American Infantry units, artillery, and supplies were already passing on the road next to the airfield, headed to Bataan province where General MacArthur planned to make a last stand.

Several years earlier, a plan was initiated that would dictate a move south should Japan attack the Philippines and leave the United States cut off from help. Called War Plan Orange-3 (WPO-3), it directed that Bataan and the fortified island of Corregidor be built up, supplied and equipped in advance to block the Japanese use of Manila Bay for a period of time. The rough jungle terrain and mountains in the center of the Bataan peninsula, and a coast that was lined with cliffs qualified the area to serve in a defensive role.[9]

Ruse was headed for the last stand of the FEAF: "We left in trucks again that night and went up into Bataan Peninsula."

This photo, dated January 28, 1942 included the inscription *"Miserable Condition of American planes after the bombing of Manila."* National Archives

We Volunteered.

CHAPTER V

BATTLE AT AGLOLOMA BAY

Immediately after this war started, the Japanese forces moved down on either side of the Philippines to numerous points south of them -- thereby completely encircling the (Islands) Philippines from north, and south, and east and west. It is that complete encirclement, with control of the air by Japanese land-based aircraft, which has prevented us from sending substantial reinforcements of men and material to the gallant defenders of the Philippines. For forty years it has always been our strategy -- a strategy born of necessity -- that in the event of a full-scale attack on the Islands by Japan, we should fight a delaying action, attempting to retire slowly into Bataan Peninsula and Corregidor. Now nothing that has occurred in the past two months has caused us to revise this basic strategy of necessity -- except that the defense put up by General MacArthur has magnificently exceeded the previous estimates of endurance, and he and his men are gaining eternal glory therefore.

Franklin Delano Roosevelt
Fireside Chat
February 23rd, 1942

Abandoning the airfield at Lubao during the night, the Squadron arrived at their destination on the Bataan Peninsula on January 2nd, 1942. "The morning found us in a heavily-wooded area on the banks of a creek in the Province of Bataan. Our first few days on Bataan were spent setting up camp. This was to be our home until our capture by the Japs on April 9th, 1942," said Ruse.

The men bivouacked in a canyon on the Bataan Peninsula at a place along a creek several-hundred yards from the road. No longer having airplanes to service, they began to prepare a new role as infantrymen. At least initially, the Squadron was reasonably supplied, but some items quickly (particularly food) began to dwindle without a means to replenish stocks. "We had cots and blankets and a lot of different supplies we had taken along with us. One of the boys, our Mess Sergeant had confiscated one whole truckload of Piedmont cigarettes, but had been able to get very little food," said Ruse. I had never seen Piedmont before, but they were made by the same tobacco company I think as Liggett & Myers that made Chesterfields. The Piedmonts were in packs of ten to a little cardboard pack. We happened to get all of these cigarettes because, the Mess Sergeant in our outfit saw the truck parked there in Manila when we were getting ready to leave Manila for the cane patch, and it was loaded full of Piedmont cigarettes. So that was one thing we had all during our stay on Bataan, even though we had run out of food and all kinds of supplies, we did have a lot of cigarettes."

As food supplies shrank, tobacco served to tide over unsatiated appetites. If they couldn't eat, at least the smokes would take the edge off of the sharp pangs of hunger in their bellies. When not working, many men spent much of their efforts just looking for something to supplement the meager diet. "The bulk of our food supply consisted of some musty, red Filipino rice which we finally learned to eat from sheer necessity. We added to our food supply by foraging around the countryside," said Ruse.

While foraging, the men became more creative about what might pass as sustenance. "We found a few wild pigs, monkeys, wild chickens, and large iguanas about four feet long," said Ruse. "In addition to these, we subsisted on bananas, mangoes, and cashew nuts, which we found in abundance. Each man had his own private cache of bananas. The stocks of bananas were cut while the fruit was still green. After being buried underground for a few days the fruit would ripen and be ready for consumption."

"One morning our Supply Sergeant, Sergeant Zeaman, came down to chow mumbling to himself and apparently in a very unhappy state of mind. After being interrogated by one of the fellows he said "Those damned monkeys got into my bananas last night. I wouldn't mind them getting my bananas so much if they wouldn't use one of my shovels to dig them up with," said Ruse.

Since the men had received no definite standing daily orders, they spent much of their spare time in wandering through the adjoining hills and gathering fruit. "I had wandered down to the road below our camp one morning headed for a nearby banana grove when I turned up the road and was passing some very dense undergrowth when I heard a rustling sound in the jungle on my left," said Ruse. "Not knowing what to expect, I stopped and threw a cartridge into the chamber of my rifle. The rustling grew louder and suddenly a little brown-skinned man about four feet tall and clad only in a breech cloth stepped into the road. He was followed by about twenty little men of the same size and color."

"Several of the men carried bows and arrows, the bows being about as long as the people were tall. The women wore a sort of skirt wrapped around their bodies from the waist down. Several of them carried babies strapped to their backs. I had heard of the Negrito people who are Negroid pygmies living in certain areas of the Philippines but these were the first I had seen," said Ruse.

The first man who Ruse encountered had appeared to be leading the way seemed to be the man in charge and seemed very excited about encountering an American. "Since they acted very friendly toward me, I approached them and started questioning them," said Ruse. "Much to my surprise the leader did speak a little broken English and said; 'Damned Japs. Too much boom boom.' All the time he was talking he kept twanging the bow string and flexing his muscles to show me what he planned to do if and when he encountered any Japs."

"After talking with the little man, I learned that Jap planes had bombed some anti-aircraft installations in the hills near their village the evening before and one bomb had fallen in the edge of the village. I gave them some cigarettes and they went on their way."

II

In the heavily-wooded area above Agloloma Bay on the high cliffs of Quinauan point, the men of the 34th Pursuit Squadron had set up four machine-gun positions using .30-caliber guns to guard against possible Japanese sea landings. On the north side of Agloloma Bay, a pair of .50-caliber guns were set up.

We Volunteered.

In the evening of January 22nd, the Japanese Imperial Army's 2nd Battalion, 20th infantry, led by Lieutenant Colonel Nariyoshi Tsunehiro, set out in eight landing barges, sailing down the coast with some nine-hundred men. Tsunehiro had been instructed to sail down the coast to Caibobo Point, and attempt to cut off the city of Mariveles on the southern tip of the peninsula, from the rest of the area. If successful, forces that had been pushed south would have no line of retreat or chance for reinforcements.

Tsunehiro had been given little time to prepare for the ambitious amphibious landing. They had little reconnaissance data to rely on, and had large-scale maps that inadequately illustrated the nuances of the coastal terrain. Their assault plan was based upon the idea that they would be able to link up with Japanese troops already advancing on the island. The division only carried enough ammunition and supplies for a few days of fighting. Traveling down the pitch-dark coast in choppy water, Tsunehiro could not pick out Caibobo point as they fought the tides in the heavy barges. The coast was made up of one steep bluff and narrow beach after another.[1] [2]

Struggling through the waters, one of the barges developed engine trouble and had to be towed by another barge. An American PT boat on patrol arrived and sank two of the troop barges, then sailed away, apparently unaware of the remaining troop barges. The attack scattered the group, which split into two squadrons, one floating about seven miles south to Longoskawayan Point, near the southern tip of Bataan, and the other group, led by Tsunehiro, not wanting to make a daytime landing, headed into a small bay under high cliffs. They had landed at Quinauan Point, a steep bit of land half a mile wide and three-quarters of a mile long.[3]

Sometime after midnight in the early hours of January 23rd, a guard on a machine-gun site at Agloloma Point spotted lights coming in from the sea around Quinauan to his north. Suspecting they were Japanese, the 34th command post was contacted, but no one there expressed concern.

The six-hundred-man Japanese Squadron made landing at Quinauan and hurriedly began to scale the rugged terrain to the top of the cliffs and immediately started entrenching themselves, digging foxholes through the dense jungle floors.[4]

A few hours later, guards on Quinauan Point were surprised to see what they thought were "Filipino" soldiers approaching them in the pitch darkness. Greetings yelled to them over a protective rock barricade were met with immediate gunfire. Rather than press forward, this Japanese amphibious landing group scaled the cliffs and went around the machine gun position. Two of the squadron's machine-gun positions had to be abandoned to the Japanese. In all of this confusion, the invaders managed to establish themselves upon a line covering about fifty yards of coast line behind American defense lines.[5] In the subsequent weeks, even more landings would be made in the vicinity on the evenings of January 26th/27th, February 1st/2nd, and 7th/8th.[6]

Prior to these amphibious landings, Ruse and those around him were still on bivouac near the Biaan River and were unsure of what their next duties would be. "We were on Bataan a few days before we found out what they were going to use us for. Our days of leisure came to an end about noon one day," said Ruse. Dyess divided the enlisted men into three platoons of about fifty men each, with each platoon assigned a non-flying officer of the squadron to conduct some hasty and impromptu infantry training.[7]

First Sergeant Royal Huston gave the enlisted men of the 21st a wake-up-call informing them of their new duties: "All right, men, this is a battle call! Grab your gear. *We aren't coming back,*" he yelled. Ruse remembers the orders he received that day: "We were told that there were many Jap snipers hidden in the trees that lined the road going up into the Bataan hills. They handed each of us a Springfield rifle and told us that we would be used to go up into Bataan behind our main lines where the Japs were landing at night and expel them from their landing sites there on the China Sea. Our first assignment as "FLYING INFANTRY" was to look for these snipers. Before leaving camp we were told that these snipers were to be found in the larger trees. They strapped themselves to the larger limbs with a wide belt and were very hard to see through the dense foliage."

After spending several days searching seeking out what was thought to be a band of advancing snipers, the men were called back into camp. Meanwhile, the Japanese forces were slowly advancing down Quinauan Point. "Captain Dyess had received orders from headquarters that we were to proceed to Quinauan Point and get the Japs out before they had a chance to infiltrate our supply routes and front line positions. Since this landing had been made behind our lines it was very essential that the Japs be liquidated," said Ruse.

Meanwhile, Filipino Scouts and Infantry had spread out in an arc along the front of Quinauan Point from Agloloma Bay. The Scouts had been tasked with shooting apart trees that may have concealed Japanese Infantry, a large task in the thick canopy of trees reaching up to seventy five feet, and bamboo so hard that .30 caliber rounds only glanced off of the wood.

It was a seven mile ride to Quinauan Point. The men were awakened after midnight during the night of January 23rd/24th loaded onto crude buses which had had their tops sawed off, and made the seven mile trip up to Quinauan where they were offloaded amid the sounds of rifle fire and blasts of mortar shell.

It was about noon when Ruse arrived and was briefed on the situation and received further orders. "We were met by a major who was back up in the trees in a Command Car, and he had a loudspeaker there. He pointed down to where the Japs were dug in and he told us that there wasn't very many of them there in the landing party; only about twenty-five to thirty, but that they were well dug-in," said Ruse.

The major said "You fellows ought to have them all out of there by night and you can go back to your bivouac there." Ruse remembers feeling optimistic at hearing this news: "When he told us this, we felt pretty good about it. We had something over two-hundred men and officers in our outfit and we felt that we had one advantage in that we were a superior force. Four days later the Filipinos behind us had buried what I once heard was about seven-hundred Japs, but I don't think it was quite that many." This was just the beginning of a long siege. "After our briefing, we began establishing our line across the point," said Ruse.

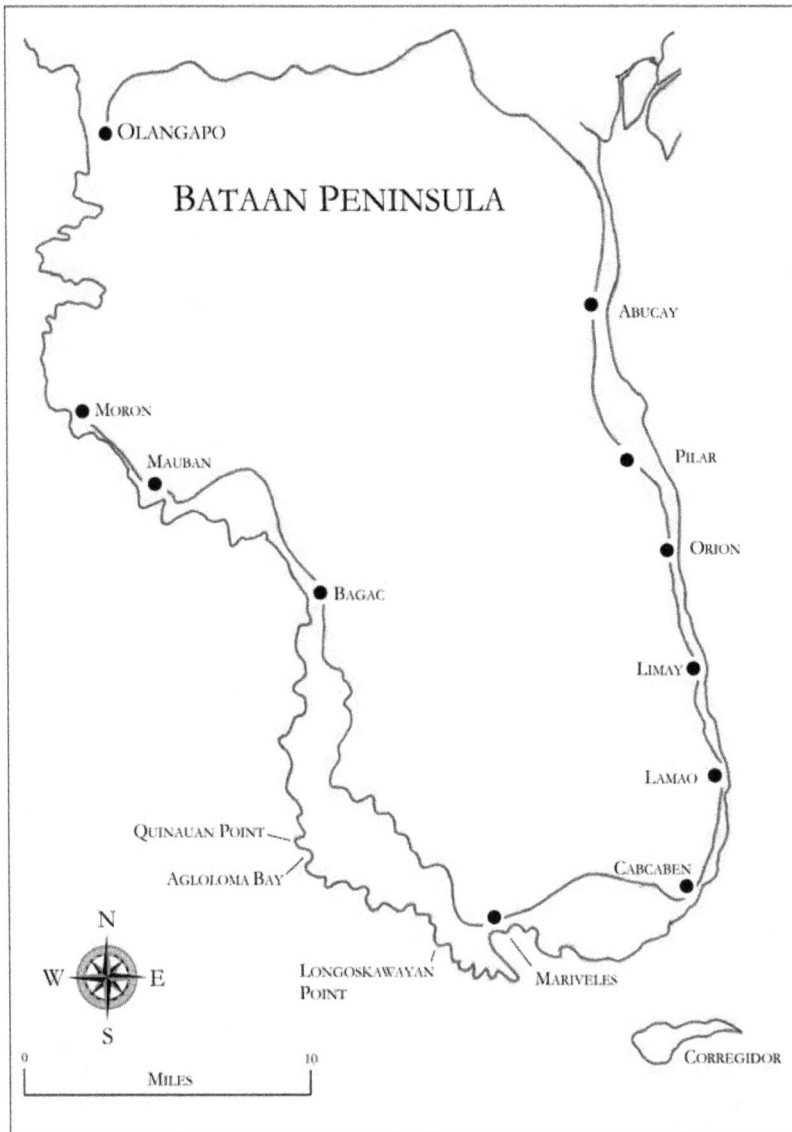

BATAAN PENINSULA

OLANGAPO

ABUCAY

MORON

MAUBAN

PILAR

ORION

BAGAC

LIMAY

LAMAO

QUINAUAN POINT

AGLOLOMA BAY

CABCABEN

N

W E

S

LONGOSKAWAYAN POINT

MARIVELES

CORREGIDOR

0 10

MILES

III

On the morning of January 25th, the 21st Pursuit was integrated with the Philippine Constabulary and Company A of the 803rd Aviation Engineers. The three units were to form a line across the thousand-yard-wide neck of the peninsula which protruded into the South China Sea between Quinauan Point and Agloloma Bay. The 21st was on the right flank, the 803rd engineers in the center, and the constabulary was on the left flank.[8]

"When we first went in there, this major told us there were two tanks that were going in there with us, as well as a few Filipino Scouts who were well acquainted with jungle warfare. Before we left Quinauan Point, we were glad we had these boys with us." At this time, the established line was only about a quarter mile from the cliffs overlooking Agloloma Bay.

Much of the jungle had already been shot away, which gave more clearance for the passage of the tanks, which were in the charge of Lieutenant John Hay. At ten o'clock, the force began advancing. First the right and left flanks would move up, then the center. The tank's fire and direction was directed at all times via walkie-talkies, as were the movements of the infantry who progressed alongside the tanks. "Hand-grenades were passed out to us and we took our positions in the line. The Japs had already started firing on us from their concealed positions ahead and I, for one, was in favor of going the opposite direction. I looked around and all the other boys were moving forward, so I just hugged the ground as close as I could and kept going," said Ruse.

The men were spaced ten to fifteen feet apart and did their best to keep their line straight as they crawled in the humid heat through the dense undergrowth through thorny and sticky vines that tore clothes and skin.

The major who had briefed the men had set up a command post to the rear and gave orders over a public address system. The infantry was told to begin advancing with the tanks slightly ahead of their line. "We did this for a short while and then he ordered us to stop and for the tanks to pull up abreast of them. I was the first man on the right of the tank that was on our left flank. The other tank was on our right flank," said Ruse.

At one point, the line began to lose shape. An officer on the top of the hill shouted, "Maintain your interval!" One of the men then yelled back. "Let the son of a bitch who gave that order try to maintain it. In a matter of seconds, one of the young pilots of the squadron came running down the hill. Following a consultation, the order was "somewhat modified".[9]

While progressing, the tanks and infantry ran into machine-gun nests that the Japanese had managed to dig-in there. The men had been told during their briefing to watch for fox-holes when they went in there. He said: "The Japs that are in there are dug-in and they'll 'play possum.' They'll lay in the fox-hole as if they are dead, and you'll get by them, and they'll either raise up and shoot you in the back or throw a hand-grenade behind you." The men were cautioned; don't advance past an enemy fox-hole without making sure its occupants were dead.

Ruse kept moving slowly alongside the tanks and advancing toward the machine gun nest. "Pretty soon one of the boys in the tank yelled out at me and said 'Mack, there's a fox-hole up ahead of you about fifty feet and I saw two Japs duck into it. Be careful when you get up there.' I really wanted to go in the other direction when I heard this, but after looking around and still seeing the others advancing, I hugged the ground and kept going. This was the first time I'd run into anything like that," said Ruse.

As the tanks slowly advanced, Ruse kept on crawling, his trajectory taking him directly toward the foxhole. He slowly made his way forward, wondering if he would be face-to-face with an enemy machine gun or bayonet when he got there. There was no place to go but forward. "When I got up to the edge, I peered over the rim of the hole there, and I had already pulled the bolt back on my Springfield, thrown a shell in the barrel and had it ready. I got up to the edge of that fox-hole, and I was about as close to the ground as I could possibly get," said Ruse.

"I peeked over the side and there was one Jap in there laying on his back with a towel on his face and I thought, 'Well, if he's dead, how in the world did he put that towel on his face?' So, I just stuck the barrel of my Springfield rifle about six inches from his head and pulled the trigger, and when I did he kind of jumped. I knew that he had been alive. And, of course, it just practically tore his head off, and blood flew all over the place. I knew he was dead then, and I was glad the major had told us about them playing possum," said Ruse.

This would not be the last time Ruse came across the enemy "playing possum." "Shortly after passing this first hole I came to another and found a Jap in it. I shot him and started around the hole when a Jap machine gun opened up about fifty yards ahead of me," said Ruse.

Upon hearing the machine gun, Ruse flattened out as low to the ground as he possibly could when he heard someone to his left yell, "Toss me a hand-grenade!"

"I had a couple of hand-grenades hanging over my belt. Sergeant Kerr from my outfit was in over to my left about ten feet," said Ruse. "He yelled over at me and said 'I can see those Japs and their machine gun up ahead.' I threw him a hand-grenade and he raised up and pulled the pin. When he raised up the machine gun opened up simultaneously. He fell back and I knew he was hit. He was dead when we got to him. I guess he was our first casualty. He never did get to throw the hand grenade because he was killed instantly."

The machine gun nest was located near one large tree that had been left standing with fox-holes dug-in all around it. "After Sergeant Kerr was killed, the tank on my left was ordered to advance toward the machine gun nest," said Ruse. "The tank moved up about fifty feet and the fire from the machine gun ceased. I took advantage of this lull and eased over to the right of the tank about twenty yards so as to get out of the line of fire. The next two fellows on my right had done the same thing and we found ourselves in a group. Having no fox-hole to get into, we stretched out flat on the ground on our stomachs facing the tank."

"There was two other fellows right there with me, one of us was a Lieutenant Jack May who lived in Arizona, and the other was a fellow named Feldman. We decided to move over to the side about fifty feet or so and lay there on our stomachs until that tank took care of the machine-gun. We got over there and were laying on our stomachs. Lieutenant May was on my left in-between

Feldman and I at about an arm's length. Feldman was about the same distance from him on his left. Either one of us could reach over and touch him."

"We were watching the tank when someone yelled 'Watch out! A Jap just ducked under the tank!' I had been watching the tank, but couldn't see anything. And then this same boy yelled 'He's getting ready to shoot!' We couldn't tell where he was going to shoot; we couldn't even see him, but then we heard this automatic rifle open up and I heard Lieutenant May on my left say 'Oooh.' I looked over at May and saw the blood was coming out of his chest and soaking his shirt. They had shot him in the chest. I told Feldman, 'We had better get him out of here.' Feldman had already checked May's pulse. 'It's too late,' Feldman said. 'It's too late. He's already dead.'"

"Looking back toward the tank, I saw a Filipino Scout run up behind it and heard him yell, 'Back up! Back up!' The tank driver, not knowing what was happening, did back up, but too slowly. The Jap crawled along underneath the tank, keeping concealed beneath the tank. The Scout ran up behind the tank and said 'Back up fast! There is a Jap under the tank!' The driver heard this and started maneuvering the tank around trying to run over the Jap with the tracks. I guess he was coming close because the Japs came from beneath the tank and ducked into a nearby fox-hole."

All afternoon the line kept advancing until the men reached a ravine that ran in from the point, in which the Japanese were heavily dug-in. The engineers in the center flank reached this area first, and suffered many casualties.

"Since darkness was approaching, we started digging in for the night. We were spaced about ten feet apart and every man was supposed to stand guard for two hours. After two hours had elapsed, the men on guard were supposed to awaken the man next to them so that they could spend two hours on guard. Nothing much happened that first night except for occasional sporadic firing from the enemy. We fired back just to let them know we were awake. I'll never forget that first night." Between guard shifts on the line, some men in the ravine spent the night injured and alive, but medics could not reach them. Rather than finish them off, the Japanese left them to scream in the darkness all through the night.[10]

We Volunteered.

"Finally the next morning, a Filipino Scout slipped up there and lobbed a hand-grenade into that machine-gun nest with him and dispensed of it. He gave us no more trouble. We went on in then," said Ruse.

"The second night up there I was spending the night in a Jap gun pit that had been knocked out. The two Japs were dead and looked like they had been dead for two or three days. They had already begun to stink the night before, and we were there on that spot all night. By morning I figured that I'd never be able to eat again, because large, green blowflies were swarming around us by the thousands all night long, and there were maggots everywhere. They had maggots all over them and they were bloated," said Ruse.

The stench of death pervaded the entire area. "I found out there's nothing that smells as bad as a human body when it's been dead several days and begins to rot; especially when the sun is as hot as it is in the Philippines," said Ruse. "I didn't think I would ever be able to eat again, but in this I was mistaken. The next morning, when our KP's finally came in and brought food to us and I sat right in between those two bloated Jap bodies and ate my food and it didn't bother me a bit. Of course, I had to fight flies with one hand and eat with the other."

On the morning of January 28th, Ed Dyess, newly promoted to Captain of the 21st Pursuit, took his men back to their camp area, being relieved temporarily by the 3rd battalion of the 45th Infantry Philippine Scouts for a brief rest and replenishment. During the battle they had eaten very little. This much needed rest lasted for six days, before the Squadron received new orders. They spent these six days bunking on the jungle floor, and without enough to eat, but this was a significant improvement over conditions at Quinauan.

After six days, the "Flying Infantry" returned to the front lines. Since they had been away, progress had been slow in the battle. The Japanese had been cleared on each flank, boxing the Japanese in on three sides, with the cliffs behind them and the sea down below. After these six days, an advance of only fifty yards had been achieved. The area was too restricted for support by artillery, and seventy-five to eighty percent of their 81-mm mortar ammunition were duds.[11]

IV

It was February 3rd when the 21st Pursuit received new orders to go back to the Quinauan Point area as reinforcements for the 45th Scouts. "Running the Japs over the cliffs had proven to be more of a task than we had bargained for. There was a drop-off of about a hundred yards down to the China Sea and we had run most of the Japs over there. There were still some of them over there that were dug-in. We spread out along the cliffs there and dug fox-holes, prepared for the night, and waited," said Ruse.

That afternoon, Dyess reported along with his men to Colonel Donald B. Hilton, executive officer of the Philippine Scouts. Hilton expressed serious concerns about the lack of infantry training among the men of the 21st, but there was little choice. Upon arrival, many of the men of the 21st exchanged their five-shot, bolt-action Springfield 1903 rifles for the Garands of the Scouts who had been killed recently, even though they were not familiar with the weapon. Grenades were delivered to the squadron as well, however, when they were picked up out of the Coca-Cola boxes they were delivered in, powder poured right out of the bottom of many of them.

After getting situated, Ruse became acquainted with some of the Filipino Scouts that were dug in near his position on the front line. "In my new position I found that there were only two men in my outfit on my left. Beyond them our line was made up of the Filipino Scouts. Since I was not acquainted with them, but had witnessed some of their methods of killing Japs, I was anxious to talk to them. Maybe it was because I had caught some of Bates' curiosity which could have been contagious. Whatever it was, I soon found myself walking over to talk to them. The first two I came to had a small fire going and were cooking some rice they had taken from the Japs. I sat back on my legs in Filipino fashion beside them and started talking," said Ruse.

"Galang, one of the two Scouts I was talking to, was about forty years old and looked about as tough as I knew he was when crossed," said Ruse. "Looking in his eyes I could also tell that here was a friend a man could depend on and one who would die fighting for what he thought was right. He asked me to stay and eat rice with them which I did mainly because I had asked him to tell me about the fighting he had seen north of Manila."

"There were over two-hundred men in my company," Galang began. "We were at Aparri when the Japs landed. I was a machine-gunner. They came at us in wave after wave. They were stacked up like cord wood in front of my gun, but still they came. I do not know how many Japs I have killed, but I have killed hundreds of them, and, if I live, I will kill more. We left most of our company at Aparri. Very few of us escaped. Now I am the only one out of my company still alive," said Galang.

"I had never seen anyone who hated the enemy as passionately as Galang, and I was glad that I was an ally of his instead of an enemy. After listening to the stories he told me about Jap treatment of Filipino civilians, especially women and children, I could easily understand his burning desire to kill Japs until there was no more to kill. Leaving Galang, I went back to my position and decided to get a little sleep since I wasn't one of the first on guard. The first night on the cliff passed rather peacefully outside of a few minor incidents," said Ruse.

At one point, the last of the Japanese soldiers retreated over the edge of the cliff. Dyess described hearing "shrieks and high pitched yelling" as "scores of Japs were tearing off their uniforms and leaping off the cliffs." Others crawled over the edge of the cliffs and down to caves and fortifications prepared on the rock ledges. Within minutes, all of the surviving Japanese were below the cliffs and out of sight. From above, the view of the narrow beach below was dotted with bodies. There were others still alive who Dyess saw "…running wildly up and down and plunging into the surf. We raked the beach and surf with machine gun fire, annihilating all who moved. Presently the waves were rolling in stained blood and dotted with dead Japs."[12]

On the morning of February 6th, Ruse and other members of the infantry attempting to end the battle by expelling the final soldiers who were fortified on the cliffs: "We tried blasting the Japs off of the side of the cliffs by lowering cases of dynamite and setting it off, but there were many caves for them to hid in, so we were unable to get them all with the dynamite." Approximately fifty Japanese were killed in one cave by using the method of lowering the fifty-pound explosive boxes with timed fuses off of the cliff, but many were unreachable in the deep caves on the narrow cliffs. After a Scout engineer was fatally wounded while lowering one of the boxes, the dynamite-method was abandoned in favor of throwing four sticks of dynamite with a thirty-second time fuse along the length of the cliffs close to the bottom edges from where the Japanese fire had come. Still, the enemy had not yet been completely exterminated and when patrols entered the area, they encountered spasmodic fire.[13]

Shortly after attempts to blast the cliffs were ceased, Captain Dyess left and didn't come back until late that evening. Colonel Hilton had received an order from General Pierce to send an officer and some men from the 21st to Mariveles to embark on a Navy craft for transport during the night to Quinauan Point to assault the cliffs from the sea.

Before leaving, Dyess stopped along the lines and told his men what was going to happen next, telling Ruse and the other men: "Hold your fire. We are going down to the naval yard at Cavite to see if they couldn't make a deal with the navy to get a boat and get a navy crew to go with them up there and get them off of that cliff." After he had gone, Ruse was approached by 2nd Lieutenant Leo B. Golden Jr., who had been left in charge. "He came down to my position and told me to get my gun and to come up to his position and spend the night. I picked up my rifle and a bandoleer of ammunition and followed him."

"Arriving at his position, I found Lieutenant McCown and another fellow waiting for us. They too were going to stay with us and we were to take turns standing watch." Lieutenant Golden informed the men that Captain Dyess had made arrangements with the Navy at Mariveles to use a few small boats equipped with machine guns and twenty millimeter guns. "He and the ten men from our outfit plus a few Navy personnel would bring the boats the next morning and attempt to blast the Japs off of that cliff from the water. We were to keep down so as not to be hit by their fire but at the same time be alert for any Japs that might try to come back up the cliffs. Since we did not want the Japs to know of our plans, it was necessary for someone to go down our lines and tell each man separately." Ruse was given this task.

We Volunteered.

After returning from telling the other men the plan for the following morning, Ruse returned to his position and learned that he was to take a shift standing guard with McCown that night. "Golden and the other fellow, whose name was Blair, were to relieve us. Blair was to be in a position about ten feet to our left and I was to walk over and awaken him when it came time for him to go on guard." After McCown and Ruse had finished their first guard shift of the night, Ruse went over to awaken Blair. "While I was gone McCown awakened Golden and then went to sleep without reminding him that I had gone over to awaken Blair."

As he approached on his return in the black of night, Ruse heard Golden's voice say, "Halt! Drop that gun!" At the same time he heard the hammer pulling back on his forty-five. "I dropped my rifle and stood motionless, knowing that he was still half asleep and might pull the trigger if I moved." After convincing him who he was, Ruse moved on in. Golden said, "Man, don't ever do that again. You'll probably never come any nearer to being shot."

McCown and Ruse went on guard again at two o'clock in the morning. "I believe that was one of the darkest nights I have ever seen in my life", Ruse said. "We were sitting there listening when we heard a faint chugging sound from out in the Manila Bay. We listened and it seemed to grow louder. About thirty minutes after we first heard it, the sound began coming to us intermittently. We decided that the Japs were sending some sort of a motor-boat or tug towing barges of reinforcements or empty barges to pick up the Japs on the beaches, and apparently they were cutting off their motor at intervals and drifting in so as not to attract too much attention. We kept listening, and it kept getting closer and closer."

Suddenly the still silence was broken and Ruse heard a strange sound coming from the Manila Bay. The sound of a shrill-screaming voice was coming in from the boat. "Whatever he said was spoken in Japanese, and the Japs below us began shooting flares. He was talking in Japanese, but it always sounded to me like he said *Joe! Papa's coming home!*"

The scream coming from the bay gave away the position of the boats in the bay, and the men opened fire from the cliff. "We had fifty caliber machine guns mounted on a point to our right and they opened up in the direction from whence the Jap had yelled," said Ruse.

From the glowing light of the tracers fired from the machine guns, Ruse could see a small tug-boat towing two empty barges which had been sent to pick up the remaining Japanese troops. "It appeared to be about three-hundred yards out and we could see it turn back out to sea, driven off by the machine gun fire. The fifty-caliber slugs evidently discouraged them because they left without making another attempt to rescue their friends on the beach," said Ruse.

As the barges were being driven back away from the beach, the Japanese soldiers were watching their last chance of escape moving back out to sea. "We had just relaxed after the barge incident when the most nerve-wracking scream I had ever heard came to us from the darkness to our left, said Ruse. "This was immediately followed by several shots from an M1 rifle. We learned that a Jap had come up over the cliff near the positions occupied by the Filipino Scouts. He was getting set to plunge his bayonet into one of the Filipino Scouts when his intended victim discovered him and grabbed him. The scream had come from the scout whose thumb was nearly bitten off by the Jap. Another Scout, awakened by the scream, came over and emptied his Garand into the Jap."

The navy supplied Dyess two whaleboats and two 35-foot longboats that had been plated with armor, and fairly early that morning, although in broad daylight, the boats came into sight, each towing a whaleboat. Meanwhile, the men above the cliffs had lowered sheets over the edge to mark the Japanese positions below. As Ruse watched, the boats approached the shore; "They came to within a hundred yards of the beach and opened fire on the Japs holding out on the cliffs." The boats maneuvered in an attack formation, slowing to avoid submerged rocks, and began blasting the areas identified by the markers hanging from above.

As the boats moved nearer to the shore, Japanese planes were spotted approaching quickly from the east, but the men on the cliffs could do little to assist those in the boats down below. "They had been firing about twenty minutes when I looked up and saw three Japanese dive-bombers fly over and start circling overhead. I wanted to warn the boys in the boat, but knowing they would be unable to hear me, I could do nothing but hope they discovered the planes in time," said Ruse. "Suddenly, the boats started moving in toward the beach, and I knew they had seen the planes. Knowing that they had little chance in the small, open boats, they jumped overboard and waded in."

The planes pointed their noses toward the bay below the cliff, and started into their first dive. "Since one of them appeared to be heading for our positions at the top of the cliff, I flattened out between the roots of a large tree nearby," said Ruse.

Once on the beach, Dyess and the men with him found some protection from strafing by hiding behind rocks on the beach. At this time, navy gunners remained on the boats and continued firing even after the one-hundred-pound fragmentation bombs began bursting all around them during subsequent passes of the dive-bombers.

Coming out of their first dive, the planes circled and started into a second dive. "This time they were dropping bombs. They dropped their bombs on the top of the cliffs where we were but their aim was bad and all but one bomb hit too far back of us to do any damage," said Ruse.

The planes made repeated passes over the area, strafing the men at the top of the cliff, as well as those on the beach and the navy boats just off shore. Ruse remained spread out on the ground between the large tree roots through the attack. "I could hear the guns and feel the impact of the bullets as they hit the ground around us. I knew they were coming close, but didn't realize that some had gone through the tree roots over my head until it was all over."

Their last bomb hit just over the cliff and right near the spot where the men had waded in from the boats. "One man was killed and several were injured; a boy named Freeland, lost both legs, and another Sergeant, Sergeant Harangody from Indiana, lost one leg[a]."

---

[a] Harangody later kept personal items for Carl Ruse so that they wouldn't not be discarded by the Japanese when he was being sent along with other healthy prisoners to Japan in 1944, and returned them to him upon their safe return to the states. Frank Harangody later became the Mayor of Whiting, Illinois.

At the beach, the gunboat was demolished by a near hit. There were casualties among the Navy personnel as well.

Despite the bombing, the shelling of the cliffs by the boats had been deadly. Only one prisoner was taken who had fled over the top of the cliff into the arms of men waiting there.

After the strafing, Ruse looked up and could hear the men just below him on the beach: "The noise from the bombs had hardly died when I heard Captain Dyess right down below me, and I'll never forget what he said. They were looking for the Japs below me and evidently they had spotted one there because I heard Dyess say to First Sergeant, Cecil Ammons. 'Go ahead and shoot him,' said Dyess. 'Don't hit that watch; I want it for a souvenir.'

V

"We had finally got our first baptism of fire, I guess, and got out of there with a few casualties. The cliffs were cleared of Japs shortly after noon and we wandered around picking up souvenirs," said Ruse. "The stench from the dead bodies was terrible, and I will never forget two Sergeants going around and collecting gold and silver teeth as souvenirs from the dead Japs. They had their pockets full."

That afternoon, with the area cleared of Japanese infantry, Ruse was given a job as a runner: "Late in the evening, Golden told me to go down the line and tell the men that we were moving out and going back to our old camp that evening. I thought several of them were going to kiss me."

Six men from the 21st had been killed during the battle. The Scout's 3rd battalion had lost seventy-four men out of four-hundred ninety-five. Four-hundred and eight Japanese were killed and six taken prisoner. Of these, three-hundred eighty-five had actually been buried by the scouts and the rest were estimated by the number of graves as buried by the Japanese, and yet others were contained in dynamited caves. A scout captain who was an American infantry officer told Dyess, "I don't know how in the world you have a man walking! You had no training in infantry and came down here like a bunch of wild Indians, and have fifteen or twenty killed or wounded and my company has only got eleven men left not killed or wounded!"

The next day, the 21ˢᵗ participated in search and cleanup operations, an unpleasant task involving removing dead Japanese from caves and other positions. The stench of the dead permeated the area, and unbearable swarms of flies surrounded them. Fortunately, the following day they were relieved of duties and went back to their old bivouac area for a much needed rest.

VI

Five years later, Colonel Hilton recalled the day he watched the men of the 21ˢᵗ march through the jungle trail past his command post. Upon their arrival, he had had great concerns in their abilities, having only basic army training and no infantry training. "I would have liked to thank each one personally for his splendid work," he reminisced.

In early February of 1942, General George visited the men, and he was presented with a Japanese saber. With it was a note that read:

> *"We, the members of the 21ˢᵗ Pursuit Squadron, who have served as engineers, infantry, artillery, anti-parachute troops, anti-sniper troops, mechanized units, marines, and air corps-our first and only love-respectfully present as a token of our esteem this Japanese saber, taken in the battle of Agloloma bay."*

As Dyess remembers the occasion, there was an additional reason for General George's visit: "He touched off a wild charivari of clanging tinware, shots, and Indian yells by letting it be known we soon would be back with our first love. The 21ˢᵗ Pursuit Squadron was assigned to Bataan and Cabcaben fields. We would be in the air again." The pilots of the 21ˢᵗ joined the remnants of several other flying organizations on February 13th. Their Philippines air force had grown from nine to ten planes, including five P-40s, an O-1 army biplane, a "ramshackle Bellanca", a dilapidated Beechcraft and a couple of other jobs" (as described by Dyess). At this time, the pilots were flying reconnaissance, moved medical supplies, and supplied men still fighting in the mountains of Luzon, as well as occasional bombing and strafing missions.

While the pilots were carrying out these missions, for many of the men of the 21st, their association with their "first love" (the air corps) had all but passed. After the battle at Quinauan Point, the majority of the men's (including Ruse) time was spent fighting as the Japanese attempted repeated their attempted troop landings. As he described it: "We'd go back to our bivouac area and whenever there would be more landings, they would send us back up there again." This is what Ruse was doing until surrender in April of 1942.

As violent battles raged on in the Philippines with limited resources, war efforts were building to a furious pace in the United States. After Pearl Harbor, FDR had decided that work on the atomic bomb must be expedited. The atomic bomb had already been evolving for over six years. In 1939, the President had been informed of the danger of the recent discovery that a chain reaction could be set up in a large mass of uranium, and that a new type of extremely powerful bombs could theoretically be constructed. It was unthinkable to have such power to fall into the hands of a brutal dictator such as Adolf Hitler.

Roosevelt responded by setting up a committee to explore the potential of the uranium atom. The committee consisted of many of the great physicists of the time, who from then on had direct access to the president for direction and resources. After the Japanese attack that drew the United States into the Pacific war, Roosevelt released emergency monies into the bomb program. In Los Alamos, New Mexico a workable weapon was to be designed under the supervision of a theoretical physicist, Julius Robert Oppenheimer. General Leslie Groves, who had recently played a key role in the construction of the enormous pentagon building in

Washington had been named as the Coordinator of the massive program and its expansive budget.[b]

VII

A war-correspondent named Frank Hewlett summed up the plight of the men on Bataan with an oft-repeated verse that became an anthem for the men there:

>*Oh, we are the battling bastards of Bataan,*
>
>*No mother, no father, no Uncle Sam*
>
>*No aunts, no uncles, no nephews, no nieces,*
>
>*No ammunition nor artillery pieces,*
>
>*And nobody gives a damn!*

While MacArthur's men were retreating further south down the peninsula towards Mariveles, Roosevelt and Churchill met in Washington in what became known as the Arcadia Conference. The meeting reaffirmed an overall "Germany First" strategy for the war. Priorities would be assigned to Europe before even the slightest hope of relief could be sent to the Philippines.

Sure enough, as early as December 28th, Roosevelt asserted that the navy was participating in an "intensive and well-planned campaign...which will result in the positive assistance of the Philippine Islands." Such assistance would be a long time in coming to the Philippine Islands.[14] Filipino President Manuel

---

[b] The cost of the atomic bomb project by the end of 1945 was $1,889,604,000. Retrieved from URL: http://www.brookings.edu/projects/archive/nucweapons/manhattan.aspx on 4-3-2010. Taken from:

Richard G. Hewlett and Oscar E. Anderson, Jr., *The New World: A History of the United States Atomic Energy Commission, Volume 1, 1939/1946* (Oak Ridge, Tennessee: U.S. AEC Technical Information Center, 1972), pp. 723-724. Includes capital and operations costs from 1942 through 1945. Costs adjusted using a base year of 1944 (the year of highest Manhattan Project expenditures).

Quezon reacted to a Roosevelt speech that focused on Europe as he watched his country in crisis from Corregidor: "I cannot stand this constant reference to England, to Europe," he shouted. "America writhes in anguish at the fate of a distant cousin, Europe, while a daughter, the Philippines, is being raped in the back room."[15]

Before the war, The Quartermaster Corps had been responsible for preparing stores of food in the Bataan Peninsula. There were immense quantities of food stored in Rizal Stadium in Manila, but it was never moved to Bataan, even though prewar plans called for a last stand of defense of the Philippines to occur on the Peninsula. Much of that food ended up falling into Japanese hands while the rations of American infantry were being cut.[16]

That February of 1942, the last horses and mules of the 26th Cavalry in the Philippines were slaughtered for food. One of the last rations drawn by Commander Dyess was "nine medium-sized cans of Salmon and forty-five pounds of musty red rice" - for one hundred seventy-five men.[17]

We Volunteered.

CHAPTER VI

DEATH MARCH FROM MARIVELES

I see no gleam of victory alluring
No chance of splendid booty or of gain
If I endure-I must go on enduring
And my reward for bearing pain-is pain
Yet, though the thrill, the zest, the hope are gone
Something within me keeps me fighting on.

Lt. Henry G. Lee
Philippine Division

In February and March of 1942, the Pilots of the 21st continued missions, which took a toll on the few remaining resources and airplanes. Of the five remaining P-40s, all had been lost except for Dyess' plane, which he named "Kibosh". After losing the four planes, one of the pilots recalled a prank note that had been written a few days before by a newspaper correspondent. Dyess had called it "ominously prophetic." Addressed to President Roosevelt, the note had read: "Dear Mr. President: Please send us another P-40. The one we have is all shot up."

Sure enough, when the crew finished work on Kibosh the next day, Dyess said that "it looked like a patchwork quilt."

We Volunteered.

On April 7th and 8th, the last remaining planes were grounded, being saved in the event that the enemy landed behind lines. On preceding nights, Japanese warships had pulled close to the bay and heavily shelled the airfield and surrounding area. On the 8th, the shelling destroyed the bivouac area where Ruse and most of the Squadron was camped. In addition, white phosphorous bombs were dropped, which set fire to the brush, causing the men to have to work as firefighters and getting no sleep. Meanwhile, a Japanese force had broken through lines and was now two miles down the road from the field. At dark, artillery at the nearest end of the field began firing on the advancing Japanese troops, now well within range. Ground crews and remaining forces began exploding ammunition stores located a quarter-mile from the field, and destroying other resources such as gasoline, radios, and guns that would have to be abandoned.

The same day, Dyess headed towards Mariveles with the remaining pilots from the 21st in a convoy that included the Ford Sedan that served as his command car and two 2-ton trucks. He had been instructed to meet three B-17s there which would fly them south. However, the travel was slow in the dark, and after midnight, the convoy ran into a traffic jam. As ammunition dumps were being exploded near the road, traffic had been brought to a standstill. Finally, Dyess arrived at Mariveles and found the runway being cleared of trucks and vehicles that had been arranged in rows of ten each on the runway, obstructing any possible landing for a B-17. When Dyess checked in, he found that the B-17s were not coming at all, but that they were to be evacuated by boat to Corregidor. When the group finally reached the boat, it was too late. A group of nurses were waiting to board the boat. The disappointed pilots waved the nurses off, and headed back to rejoin the enlisted men at Mariveles, having no other means of transportation.[1]

II

Ruse, an enlisted man, had not had any hope for evacuation by plane, boat, or any other means. While men on Bataan fought to defend their line, eating shrinking rice rations and whatever other food they could forage for, Douglas MacArthur had been on the heavily-fortified island of Corregidor since Christmas Eve. Because of his rare appearances outside of the tunnels in the rock of Corregidor, he had began to be known as "Dugout Doug" on Bataan. While MacArthur was known for his physical courage, it is speculated that his reason for not returning from Corregidor more frequently than he did was not because he was afraid for his safety, but because, "he could not look his doomed men in the eye."[a]

In March of 1942, following direct orders from Roosevelt, MacArthur left Corregidor and Bataan, leaving General Jonathan Wainwright as the new commander of the Philippines. At this time, Ned King became the commander of the men on front line of the battlefield in Bataan.

MacArthur, upon arriving in Australia famously explained to reporters in a press conference that he had left the Philippines upon Roosevelt's orders: "For the purpose, as I understand it, of organizing the American offensive against Japan, a primary object of which is the relief of the Philippines. I came through and *I shall return.*"

When MacArthur finished his press conference, he met with one of his staff officers to be briefed on the situation after his travels. To his amazement, no relief force had been gathered at all.[2]

Meanwhile, Ned King was in the Philippines on the front lines with his men. The troops that King commanded were malnourished and in poor fighting condition with no chance of reinforcements, and as March turned to April, the battle lines

---

[a] Richard Frank, in his biography of MacArthur notes this distinction of MacArthur, specifically saying the following of his rare return appearances to Bataan from Corregidor: "The most likely, though speculative, explanation for this is that MacArthur's physical courage (or fatalism) transcended his moral courage. He could not look his doomed men in the eye."

continued to be pushed back and fragmented while the huge Japanese force pushed its way down the peninsula.

King was soon in a position where he would have to decide whether there was any reason in continuing the fight any longer. By mid day on April 8th, he had made up his mind. The line had broken, and the Japanese were only a few miles from a large army field hospital with six thousand sick and wounded, and twenty six thousand civilians.[3]

At midnight, King assembled his headquarters and staff to inform them of the surrender.

> "I did not ask you here to get your opinion or advice. I do not want any of you saddled with any part of the responsibility for the ignominious decision I feel forced to make. I have not communicated with General Wainright [directly] because I do not want him to be compelled to assume any part of the responsibility. I am sending forward a flag of truce at daybreak to ask for terms of surrender. I feel that further resistance would only uselessly waste human life. Already [one of] our hospital[s], which is filled to capacity and directly in the line of hostile approach is within range of enemy light artillery. We have no further means of organized resistance."

At 9:00 A.M. on April 9th, a surrender party set out in two jeeps, each with a white bed sheet flying from a bamboo pole. In the first jeep was the operations officer, Colonel James V. Collier, and a junior officer who was guiding the group. In the second jeep was King and two of his aides. Driving on the National Road, a flight of Japanese fighters swooped down and began strafing the jeeps, causing them to have to jump for cover. The intermittent strafing lasted over an hour.

The group traveled for over two hours, making it well-past their own front lines. Rounding a turn in the road near the Lamao River Bridge, a platoon of Japanese infantry jumped into the road and surrounded the party, signaling them to stop with bayonets drawn. King met with Colonel Motoo Nakayama, senior operations officer of the 14th army, making it clear that he commanded troops on the Bataan peninsula only, not Corregidor or the southern Philippine islands. Having no success in attempting to negotiate terms, King agreed to an unconditional surrender of his men.[4] He had faced the facts, knowing he could even be court-martialed after the war; however, the situation had become hopeless on the Bataan Peninsula. King was taking a chance that the enemy would honor the Geneva Convention, though they had never signed it.[5]

On April 9th, 1942 Ruse was near Mariveles Airfield with Cpl. Robert L. Greenman from the 21st. Greenman was known among the men in the 21st, as an accomplished concert pianist, who had played for the men on the voyage to the Philippines aboard the *President Coolidge*, and played on occasion on a salvaged piano which was a great morale-boost for the men. Greenman had lost a finger during the 21st Pursuit's first trip into battle at Quinauan. "While we were down there, we were on guard-duty, and Greenman got sick; he came down with Malaria; one of the worst diseases there is, in my opinion. The sickest I have ever, ever been was when I had malaria. We had been given orders that we were to meet back at our old bivouac up there at the creek in Bataan. We started back up there, and Greenman was so sick I had to help him along, and I had to carry his rifle and mine too," said Ruse.

Ruse and Greenman started out on the Bataan National Road: "I decided we'd go along over the roads going up into Bataan. When we'd get on the road it would be easier walking. We got over there where we could see what was going on, and the road was jammed with troops, soldiers, and civilians. And the Japs were strafing them over there. Even though the war was about to end, they were still strafing them, so we decided that wasn't a very healthy place to be. I told Greenman we could go back over and find the creek and follow the creek back to our old bivouac area," said Ruse.

Later that day, Ruse and Greenman arrived at Mariveles Airfield where they learned that they had been surrendered by King to the Imperial Japanese Army. "We met down there and they told us that General King had surrendered us. He spoke to us and told us to not feel bad about the surrender because we weren't the ones who had surrendered, he surrendered for us." The men in each unit had been instructed to pile their few remaining arms and munitions in a mound, and place a white flag on top.

We Volunteered.

King discusses terms of surrender with Motoo Nakayama. National Archives

When Dyess heard of the surrender he was furious. Despite obvious signs being given that the forces would surrender, the Japanese were still attacking disarmed American and Filipino troops. Dyess suspended his plans to rejoin his men at Mariveles, feeling that it was every man for himself now. He did not want to surrender to these barbarous people. He said to the group of pilots, "I know where there is a boat. A guy named Tex Marable has it and will let me have it!" However, Marable, who had recently become the Commanding Officer of the 17th Pursuit, which was still on beach defense, refused to hand over his boat to the men. With no hopes for a boat, Dyess told the men to find their Squadrons so that they would be present when the surrender formalities began.

Dyess reached headquarters with Grashio, and Bob Ibold, and learned that the surrender had gone through. The group then headed towards Mariveles in the command car. At one point, the group came face to face with two Japanese tanks. The pilots got out of the car, holding up white handkerchiefs. They were motioned closer by a Japanese standing on the nose of the lead tank, but when they started moving, they were stopped and he made a motion to drive closer. They got back in the car and drove up to the tank. Then the Japanese yelled at them in English, "You Americans can't be trusted. You surrender but you do not give up your arms!" The men had forgotten that they were still wearing their .45s, now dropping them aside and raising their hands. The Japanese soldier then slapped Dyess' face. Another Japanese soldier told Grashio to give him his ring, fountain pen, watch, pencil and bracelet, then motioned them to get back in the car and continue to their unit. Looking back, Grashio saw the man sneer at him and throw his things back into the car.[6][7]

Meanwhile, the 21st's men had congregated at kilometer post 181 along Bataan's major artery, the Old National Road, stacking their weapons in piles.[8] The road consisted of two lanes made of gravel and dirt in some areas, and blacktops the rest of the way. The road began at Mariveles and headed north by the bay up to Hermosa, cutting through most of Bataan's towns along the way.

After several days with no rest, that night, the men finally slept and were awakened early the next day by Japanese Guards.

They were lead to the airstrip north of Mariveles and arranged in lines. Dyess recalled men being instructed to get rid of any souvenirs or materials with Japanese connections. Possessions were searched on the spot, some personal articles were confiscated. As Dyess described it, some men were beaten or murdered for being caught with "some Japanese trifle."

The Japanese were surprised and unprepared for such a large surrender. Ritual suicide or "hari-kiri", literally meaning "stomach cut" was a voluntary disembowelment that was frequently done to avoid shame or the dishonor of capture by an enemy. The individual would make a long cut across their own stomach. The method was culturally considered to display courage because it was a slow and painful death, and as they saw it, showed courage.

In a culture that preferred death over capture, the Japanese were suddenly overwhelmed by thousands of prisoners who, in their eyes, had dishonored themselves by surrendering and not ending their own lives. The surviving POWs would endure pain far greater and far longer lasting than a relatively quick suicide, and were driven by a truer courage and stubborn grit and determination to survive despite horrible circumstances and for potentially far greater epochs of time than a quick suicide would ever afford a Japanese soldier.

From his headquarters in Australia, General MacArthur paid homage to the Battling Bastards of Bataan, heard by their families at home: "No army has ever done so much with so little."[9]

III

At the time that the Bataan Death March began, only one-hundred and sixty officers and men remained in the 21st Pursuit Squadron. Many of them were already half-starved. "The Bataan Death March was a good name for that march because a lot of the boys were killed on that death march. They were either bayoneted or had their heads chopped off. We found out then that the Japs were the most sadistic people we'd ever seen and probably ever would see. It was the worst situation I've *ever* been in because we were at the mercy of the Japs. Maybe a Jap wouldn't like the looks of one of the boys would run a bayonet through him or something like that for no reason at all. They were the worst people I've ever been around. They'd kill boys. They'd find a souvenir on them or something like Japanese money or something like that, and they'd kill 'em. They wouldn't ask any questions. If someone fell out of the march because they got too weak to walk they'd either bayonet 'em, or they even had gone as far as to chop their head off right there in front of us. Some of the worst things I ever saw in my life happened for no reason."

"The last two months we were on Bataan we didn't have any food. I never ate a monkey, but I ate lizards. We soon had ate all of the bananas and wild fruit that grew there. And we ate all of the cavalry mules. So, we were pretty weak to start with," said Ruse.

"A lot of the fellows couldn't walk. It was eighty miles, that march, eighty miles with no food, and, a lot of the fellows couldn't hold up, but their buddies would try to carry them or help them along. We had no water although there were Artesian wells all along the road going out of Bataan, but the Japs wouldn't let us drink," said Ruse.

"A lot of people got killed just trying to get a drink of water. One time, they let me and a group that I was in, go over and drink out of a pool of water. We got over there and we could see why they let us drink; there was an old dead, bloated horse in this water. We went ahead and drank it," said Ruse.

Finally, the men were allowed to rest, but only for a brief period. "We finally got to rest a little one night a little bit along the road. We just had to lay down on the road and sleep. We didn't get to rest very long because they got us back on our feet and got us to marching," said Ruse.

During the rest break, Ruse witnessed the guards attempt to bury men alive. "There was four Filipinos, and they made them dig a big hole, and after they had gotten the hole dug to their satisfaction, the Japs pushed 'em in it and started covering 'em up. Of course these Filipinos kept trying to get out, and the Japs would hit 'em with a rifle butt," said Ruse. Finally, they got 'em buried. They knocked 'em out and got 'em buried. That's one of the many things they were capable of doing and did do during that march."

"I think probably the worst thing I saw on this march was when Filipino civilians would be standing alongside the road and we would go through these little "Barrios" or towns where these people lived. There was one Filipino lady standing there holding a baby and a Jap soldier took the baby out of her arms and threw it up in the air and caught it on his bayonet. But, it just kind of shows you what we were up against. We had no idea when we surrendered what kind of people they were. They didn't abide by the Geneva Convention or anything. They did whatever they wanted to do with their prisoners. I don't have any idea how many boys died, most were killed, on the march out of Bataan," said Ruse.

The Survivors of the march eventually arrived at San Fernando and were placed in a barbed-wire enclosure there that could only accommodate all of the men by forcing them to stand up while packed in there. Ruse remembers being given the first food he had received on the march in San Fernando. "We had to stand up for a day and finally they gave us a ball of rice about the size of a baseball. That was the first food we had had on the march." It was now April 13th; the fourth day of the march.

Dyess recalled that, in addition to being crowded, the compound was filthy due to the condition of the men, and the lack of any functional sanitary facilities whatsoever: "The stench of the place reached us long before we entered it. Hundreds of the prisoners were suffering from dysentery. Human waste covered the ground. The shanty that was used as a latrine was no longer usable as such. Maggots were in sight everywhere. There was no room to lie down. We tried to sleep sitting up, but the aches of exhaustion seemed to have penetrated even into our bones."

After two additional days of marching, the prisoners were put on a freight train inside, small, poorly ventilated wooden boxcars with narrow screened slits at each end. The cramped railroad cars were a squat 33' x 8' and 7' high and packed with one hundred to one-hundred and fifteen men.[10] The old World War I era boxcars were referred to as "Forty and Eights," so nicknamed because they were designed to hold forty men or eight horses.[11] "They crowded us in there so tightly that we couldn't sit down or lay down or anything. A lot of these boys were right on the verge of death anyway, and when somebody died, about the only thing we could do was just pass them overhead to the fellows by the door. The only thing they could do was toss them out the door," said Ruse.

The sweltering-hot train ride took over four hours to navigate twenty five miles, where the men were finally able to get off of the train.[12] "We finally got over to a place called "Capas", and the Filipino civilians were lined up there along the street with all kinds of food for us, and for some reason, the Japs let them feed us. That's the first time we had really eaten in probably six days. After we had eaten we started on our march to our first prison camp which was Camp O'Donnell. As well as I remember, O'Donnell was somewhere around five miles from Capas." Ruse had survived what would come to be known as one of the most horrendous war-crimes ever suffered by American Soldiers. As many as ten-thousand Americans and Filipinos died during the event that the men referred to at the time simply as "the Hike."[13]

IV

Dyess remembered seeing Camp O'Donnell for the first time as: "A maze of tumbledown buildings, barbed wire entanglements, and high guard towers, from which flew the Jap flag. The camp covered a wide area, probably several hundred acres. The road by which we had entered bisected it in the center. Lesser roads branched off to the north and south. The main road was flanked by barbed wire entanglements." O'Donnell was built to house nine thousand men, but the Japanese would cram fifty thousand prisoners into the rudimentary facility.

After walking through the gates of O'Donnell, the men were lined up for a "sun treatment" outside of the barracks, where the prisoners were subjected to the first of many rambling, vicious and arrogant speeches from Captain Yoshio Tsuneyoshi, the camp's commandant.[14]

When Tsuneyoshi was satisfied with the lashing, he stomped down from his platform. "We got into O'Donnell and got put in an old Filipino Army barracks in an old Filipino Army camp," said Ruse. "They had a nipa barracks there where they would take strips of bamboo and make floors. They had bays in their made of strips of bamboo where we would sleep. We had no sanitary facilities whatsoever. They had what we called "straddle trenches" where we had to go to relieve ourselves, and it wasn't but just a short time till the flies and maggots took over. Some of those boys would get so weak from dysentery, and beriberi, and malaria that they couldn't hold themselves up. They would get out to that latrine and one of them would fall in and have to be helped out. Some fellows would get down there and just couldn't get out. Just lay there among those maggots and flies. You can imagine what it would be like to fall into a bunch of maggots and human waste and not be able to get yourself out, and then have no way to clean up after you got out of there. They had one hydrant in the whole camp and we would line up there for days to fill our canteen," said Ruse.

The filth that was in most of the camp was also present in the kitchens, which were typically shacks with dirt floors, alive with the same flies and mosquitoes as the rest of the camp. Water for cleaning cooking utensils was not present in the kitchen. Clothing would commonly go unwashed for months at a time, and bathing was not a possibility. A stream that made its way through the camp had quickly become befouled by the dysentery epidemic. During the final days at O'Donnell, rains came and washed out the stream, allowing the rinsing of clothing and for bathing.

After a short time at the filthy camp, Ruse found himself to be in what he considered a fortunate position; he was able to leave O'Donnell with a work detail. "We were there just a short time (maybe about two weeks) when they took a group of us back up to Bataan on a detail to recover a bunch of cars and trucks and buses that we had tried to destroy before the surrender. A lot of them were run off of the road up there in the hills, and a lot of them were in still-running condition. They wanted to pull them back up on the road so they could tow 'em to San Fernando to be shipped to Japan to be used for parts in their war efforts. We didn't have time to really destroy them so we just ran them off the road. I've forgotten how many men there was on this detail, but we had a lot of Jap cars with us and they would put us in a truck in the morning and start out and go find a truck or a car or a bus off the road and pull it back up on the road," said Ruse.

"The second day I was out they put me in a big old Autocar diesel. It had a big winch on the front of it. The two Jap guards that were with me jumped off of the truck and we got up on the side road up there in Bataan and it was muddy. It had been raining and it was right on the edge of a pretty steep bank. There was big trees growing down there and there was two buses down there butted up together end to end," said Ruse.

The guards stopped the diesel above the buses, with the plan to retrieve them and pull them up on the road. "They got out and motioned me to let the slack out on the winch and I did. We got enough slack, and instead of hooking onto the bus closest to us, they hooked onto the bus furthest away which was butted up against the other. I started taking out the slack like he told me to, but it couldn't move both buses and that truck on that muddy road started slipping sideways. They kept motioning for me to take up slack and I did, but I knew what was going to happen," said Ruse.

The winch turned over, winding the cable onto the spool. Ruse slowed the winch, but the captors motioned him to keep pulling the cable. All the while Ruse sat in the truck as the old diesel was slipping ever closer to the edge of the hill on the thick mud. "When the truck got to where I knew it was going to go over the bank I jumped out," said Ruse.

The Autocar slid off of the road and tumbled down the hill towards the buses and the guards. The guards were furious, at the loss of the truck, which they were responsible, and Ruse found himself as the scapegoat. When they met him at the road, the beating began. "I guess that was one of the worst beatings I ever got," said Ruse. "They had to do something to save face because if they had to go back to camp and tell their superiors that they had lost the truck, they would have been in a lot of trouble. So they blamed me for it so I could take the blame."

"The Japs are funny people. The non-coms would beat up on the privates; officers would beat up on the non-coms. They wouldn't just chew 'em out for something they did wrong or maybe something they didn't do wrong; they had just decided they wanted to get on 'em about something. I've seen 'em knock 'em clear across eight or ten feet with their fists. Especially when they were full of sake," said Ruse.

"Finally, (I don't recall how many days we were up there on Bataan recovering those vehicles, perhaps about two weeks), but we finally left and went back to the prison camp," said Ruse

Working conditions on the auto detail were an improvement only in that they put distance between Ruse and the filth in Camp O'Donnell, and the work-details in the camp. The endurance needed for such work and brutal treatments was been tremendous. Ed Dyess recalls circumstances of labor details after only a month at O'Donnell in the following way: "The prisoners were organized into two companies of two hundred each with an American officer at its head. The officers went along with the men, but were not allowed to supervise the work. If we could have assigned the men to the tasks, sparing the enfeebled soldiers and shifting the heavier work to the stronger ones, we might have been able to save many lives. But we were used chiefly as interpreters and as butts for the jokes, insults, and abuse of the Japs. By May 15th, a month after our internment at O'Donnell, less than twenty men of each company were able to go on detail and not many of these were able to labor in the equatorial sun."

Despite the terrible conditions all around, a theme in Ruse' time as a prisoner of the Japanese was relative health and stubborn endurance. When men were dying all around him, he found himself continuing to work and continuing to be placed on details. Despite sickness and injury, he endured it all and evaded death that was falling many brave and strong men all around him. In two months at O'Donnell more than 2,200 POWs died.

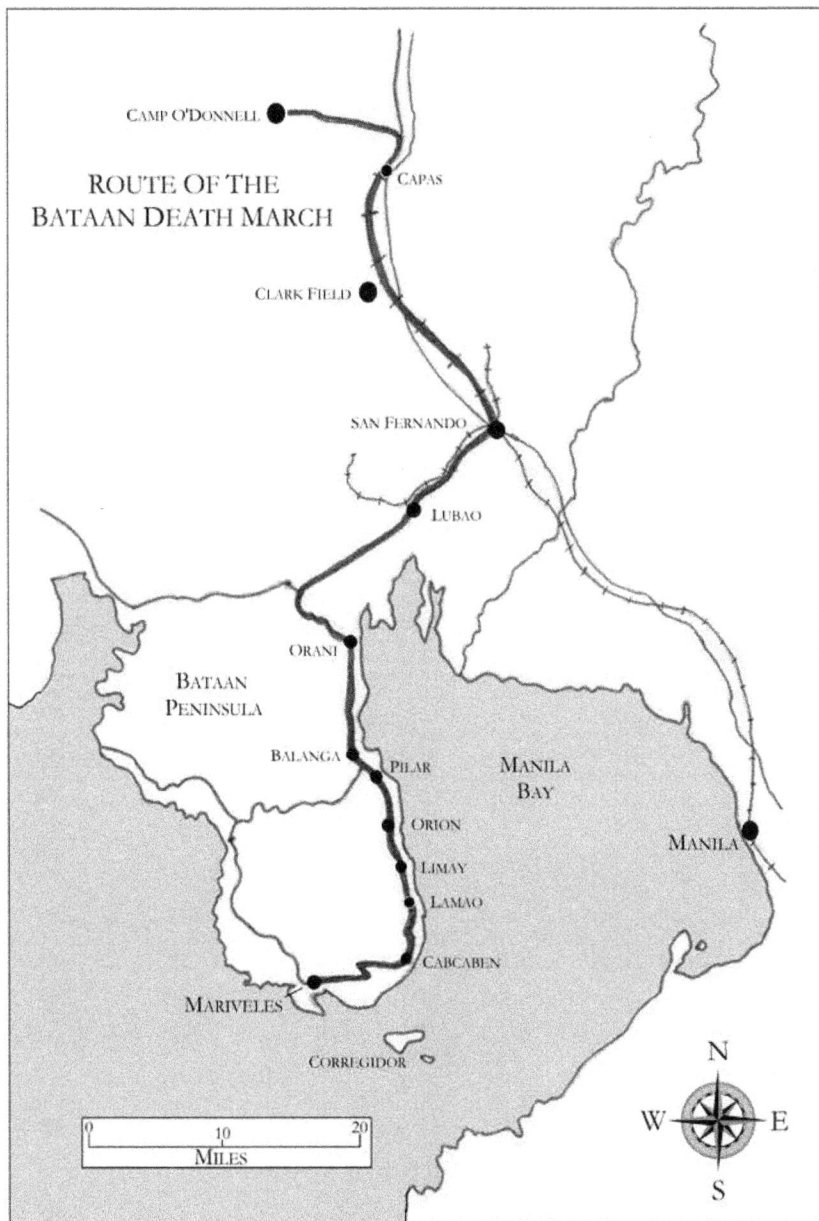

ROUTE OF THE
BATAAN DEATH MARCH

CAMP O'DONNELL
CAPAS
CLARK FIELD
SAN FERNANDO
LUBAO
ORANI
BATAAN
PENINSULA
BALANGA
PILAR
ORION
LIMAY
LAMAO
CABCABEN
MANILA
BAY
MANILA
MARIVELES
CORREGIDOR

0   10   20
MILES

N
W   E
S

CHAPTER VII

BURIAL DETAIL

I have no peace, no quietness; I have no rest, but only turmoil.

JOB 3:26

In Arlington, Virginia in May, the weather is perfect. On the shaded green hillside lawns that surround the former home of Robert E. Lee, the view is immense. Looking east and gazing downhill, there is a view that compels the observer to *stand* in order to take in the solemn and beautiful view with an appropriate deference; to *sit* down to take it in would be an act of irreverence; an insult to the place. No, one must stand to take it in. The blue sky reflects on the Potomac River as it seeps on by. Looking down from the sandstone columns of the Confederate General's front porch, the eyes follow the granite arches of the Memorial Bridge that connect a straight line between the old house and the Lincoln Memorial in a dramatic and symbolically appropriate representation of the reunification of the nation after the Civil War. A mile beyond Lincoln's dignified white columns, the observer sees the white obelisk monument to the life of George Washington, and another mile away is the dome of the U.S. Capitol.

Standing in the spot in May of 1942, the observer's eye would be drawn to their right, as the circular colonnade and white dome were being constructed under which a bronze, larger than life Thomas Jefferson looked north, directly into the windows of the oval office, keeping a watchful eye on the tenant of the old house on Pennsylvania Avenue. Looking further to the right, the eye could not overlook the expansive Pentagon, with its finishing touches being completed after a whirlwind wartime construction. From Lee's lawn, all of the views were dramatic and beautiful, but most of all, the eye was drawn just below the old house, where endless rows of white, uniform marble tombstones stretched over hill after hill. It was, in fact, a beautiful place for a funeral.

Each day, flag-draped coffins would lead processions of mourners down oak-lined lanes to a final resting place. During World War II, the United States lost over four hundred thousand citizens, causing the number of daily burials to increase, and eventually creating a need for an expansion of the cemetery.

The funerals went on with the highest reverence in the sacred and beautiful place in a display of the nation's patriotism, and our best attempt to honor those who made immense sacrifices in service of country. At Arlington, everything seemed to emanate reverence; the sky, the calmly rolling hills, the dignified architecture, the tranquil quiet. Meanwhile, in warzones in Europe and in the Pacific, men were meeting violent deaths each day, with no ceremony to even attempt to do justice to their great sacrifice.

II

While away on the auto recovery detail, prisoners at Camp O'Donnell had been moved to Cabanatuan number one. Upon his arrival, Ruse discovered similar living conditions than those at Camp O'Donnell, with rampant sickness and starvation killing men every hour of the day. Similar latrines as used at O'Donnell, mosquitoes, and a lack of sanitary facilities continued to cause widespread disease such as malaria, dysentery, and beriberi. Heat exhaustion and abuse were other common causes of death. "The conditions there were no better than they were at O'Donnell. The boys were dying at a rate of maybe fifty a day. I was on grave-digging details in the morning," said Ruse. "We would go out and dig a long trench. In the afternoon we had a burial detail. We'd take a bamboo pole between two men and tie these corpse wrists together and their ankles together, and run this bamboo pole in-between there. We'd put the pole on our shoulder and carry them out to the graves and put them in that trench just like cordwood. Then we'd cover them up. During the rainy season, we'd go down the next day after we'd buried a bunch, and legs and arms would be sticking up out of the ground and dogs would be eating on them."

Cabanatuan had a Japanese army camp and hospital area on one side, and a prison section that was separated from the rest by barbed wire. Along the east side of the camp were three guard towers with machine guns, with the Japanese flag at the top. There were three buildings for the prisoners, and the prisoners had named the roads that snaked between them. There was a Broadway, Main Street, Market Street, and Michigan Avenue, among others. One man named a street after himself; "Buboltz Boulevard" led to the camp latrines. Cabanatuan was expanded over time to three separate camps, but Ruse spent all of his time in Cabanatuan before being transferred. As he put it: "I had another streak of luck."

III

On October 24th, 1942 Ruse was placed in a group of approximately one thousand men who were to be shipped to the Island of Mindanao, the southernmost island in the Philippine group. The Japanese had wanted a group of one thousand "literate laborers", to be taken to a place where they would have regular work. While there was risk involved in leaving, many of the men felt that it would be worth it to get out of Cabanatuan.[1] In less than six months since their surrender, nearly three thousand POWs had died. The risk, it seemed, was a necessary one. Ed Dyess signed up to go. His men followed his lead.

The men were fed before dawn and assembled into groups of one hundred with full packs.[2] They were marched out the gates as those who stayed behind waved final goodbyes from inside the barbed wire fence. It was a four mile hike to the town of Cabanatuan where the men were loaded into narrow gauge boxcars similar to those that had taken them from San Fernando to Capas and set off to Manila. This time the trip was better, with only about eighty men per boxcar as opposed to one hundred plus that made the trip in the cars the first time. During the hike, a rainstorm soaked the men and their packs, but it was refreshing, and cooling once they were in the metal boxcars.[3]

That night the prisoners were marched through the streets to Bilibid Prison where they slept on concrete floors. The next day, October 25th, they were awoken and marched by their Japanese captors through the streets of Manila for what many of them thought was a "victory march"; a display intended by the Japanese to affect the morale of the Filipino citizens. Dyess recalled their reception on the march: "The Filipinos who lined the streets looked at us silently and with compassion. The women wept openly. Wherever we looked, people were covertly making the V for Victory sign. From the Jap point of view, the march was a flop. The attitude of the populace discouraged even the Jap soldiers who stood here and there along the streets."

It was evening when the company Ruse was marching with arrived at the at the seaside docks. Their ride was a four hundred foot, 7,000-ton British-built vessel, the *Erie Maru*[a] that had been refitted as a Japanese troopship and later a combination cargo and convict ship. The captors had neglected to mark the Japanese merchant ship as carrying prisoners of war, potentially making it an attractive target for any submarine that might find it in its periscope.

"We got on this old Jap boat, to make the trip from Manila to Davao Penal Colony," said Ruse. Dyess was surprised at the

---

[a] The *Erie Maru* was torpedoed in 1944. Retrieved from URL: http://www.west-point.org/family/japanese-pow/ShipsAlpha.htm on 5-14-10

conditions aboard on his first sight of the ship: "I think it must have been the filthiest vessel ever to put to sea. The deck was heaped with goods and junk of all kinds. The hold in which we were to sleep smelled almost as bad as the hospitals at O'Donnell and Cabanatuan. Areas had been boxed off throughout the hold, and twelve men were assigned to each. There was room for only six to sleep at one time. The Jap troops had left millions of lice and bedbugs, and in a few hours we were crawling with them." Below the decking of the ship, the Japanese had added a large quantity of gasoline, which added to the already-foul smell."[4] The sleeping quarters consisted of decks three feet high were partitioned into compartments five feet wide and ten feet deep.[5]

"En route to Davao, we stopped at Cebu.[b] I don't know what we stopped there for, but during our stay there, the Japs gave us some rice for our cooks to cook for us. It was rice that had been cleaned out of a warehouse that had been bombed by American planes, and there were little slivers of glass all through it because it blew the windows out of the warehouse they were in. And they gave the rice to us. Of course, the cooks tried to get rid of most of the glass, but before we could eat the rice we had to kind of feel around with our tongue to make sure there was no glass in there and we'd spit the glass out. I don't think anyone died from eating glass, but we had a hard time eating", said Ruse.

Ruse would spend ten days in the ship to Davao, losing track of time during the long and monotonous passage: "We loaded on the boat again and started on the rest of our journey to Davao. In a situation like that you don't keep track of time, or I didn't keep track of time. All I knew was the difference between day and night."

During the voyage, there were rumors of mutiny by the men down in the hold of the ship. American and Filipino prisoners on the ship outnumbered the Japanese significantly, but in the end the men decided against any attempts at overthrowing their captors. Even if they were successful, what would they do next? The ship was unmarked as carrying POWs, so there would be a threat of being torpedoed by submarines if the ship were to venture out into

[b] In his memoir, Ed Dyess recalled that this stop was at Iloilo, near Cebu.

open water. Additionally, the Japanese would most certainly get a radio message out before being subdued. Eventually, the hopes of escape faded, and the plans to take the ship over died.[6]

IV

It was November 7th, two weeks after leaving Cabanatuan when the boat arrived at the pier of the Lasang Lumber Company in Davao. After disembarking, the men were subjected to several hours of sun treatment near the pier, and then took their lunch of rice and picked cherries and were ordered to their feet.[7] Ruse was loaded on a truck and arrived at Davao Penal Colony at near 2:00 A.M. He would be incarcerated there for two years; the majority of his term as prisoner of the Japanese.[c]

Upon arrival at his new home, Major Kazuo Maeda, commander of the camp, inspected his new workforce. Dyess described his reaction as one of disappointment: "He had asked for laborers, not scarecrows."

Maeda stood ahead of the men as he often did, on a platform to offset his short five-foot frame, and with his single gold-tooth shining in the sun. Maeda had been a 1910 graduate of the Imperial Army Academy at Ichigaya, yet, due to his proclivity towards alcoholic beverages, he tended towards solitude, which showed up in his rare, disheveled appearances.[8]

---

[c] Having been placed on a truck may indicate that Ruse was ill upon arrival to Davao after the ride from Cabanatuan. In his memoir, Ed Dyess states that some men were expected to march to the prison. He states: "Men who had been sick aboard the ship began falling out soon after the march began. Since they were intended as laborers, however, they were placed in the trucks that moved along with us. But not until Captain Hosume, in charge of the guards, had seen to it that they were thoroughly boxed and mauled. Hosume did not approve of the rest periods which were granted, nor did he think it right that a water truck had been brought along so that we might quench our thirst as often as necessary. These comforts probably were what aroused him to order savage beatings for those who fell out." In Lukacs, 2010, the author states that only 300 of 1000 prisoners made the entire 27 kilometer trip to Davao on foot.

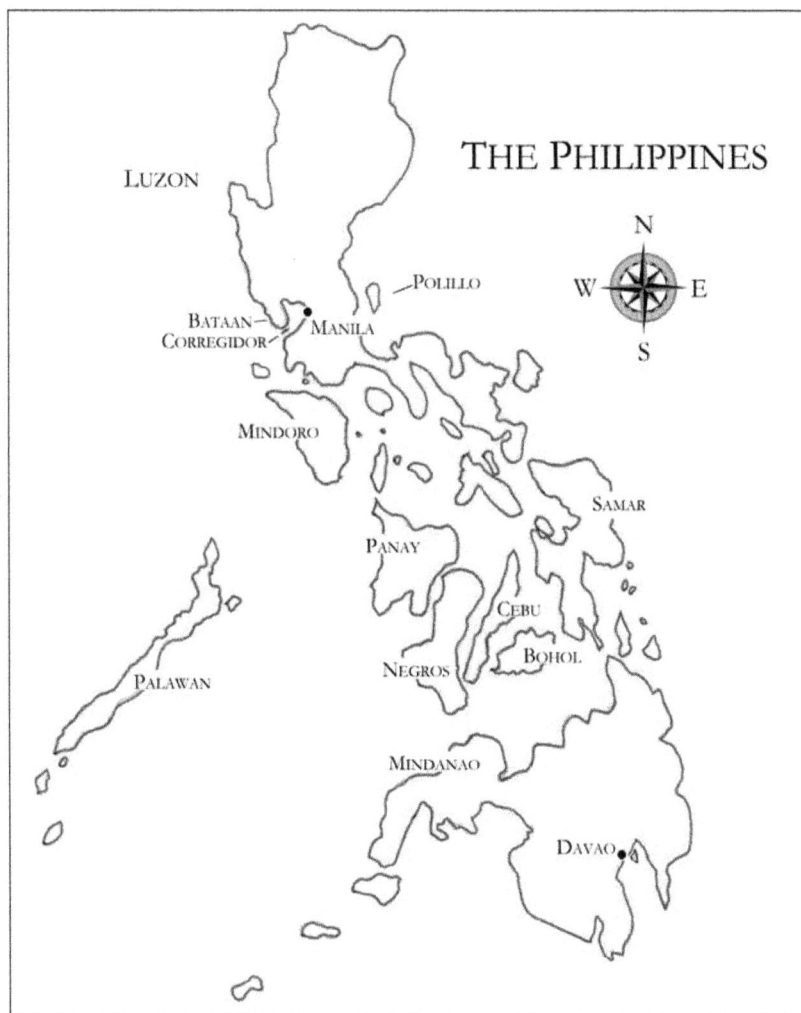

THE PHILIPPINES

LUZON

POLILLO

BATAAN
CORREGIDOR
MANILA

MINDORO

SAMAR

PANAY

CEBU

NEGROS
BOHOL

PALAWAN

MINDANAO

DAVAO

CHAPTER VIII

DAVAO

Not gold, but only men can make
A nation great and strong;
Men who for truth and honor's sake,
Stand fast and SUFFER LONG.

Brave men who work while others sleep,
Who dare while other's shy,
They build a nation's pillars deep,
And lift them to the sky.
                              — *Ralph Waldo Emerson*

rison quarters at Davao sat in a ten acre compound surrounded by double walls of barbed wire with a walking patrol constantly moving in between. There were guard towers around the perimeter. Nine parallel buildings about fifty to sixty feet apart and one hundred fifty feet long by sixteen feet wide served as barracks, and across the road to the east were Japanese headquarters. The camp was situated on a slight rise in the terrain that was surrounded by thick jungle.[1] The barracks were built on piers approximately two feet high, and had galvanized tin roofs. Walking through the door, an aisle about five feet wide ran the length of the barracks, with a sleeping platform extending out to the exterior wall that ran the length of the barracks. The entire camp was enclosed by two fences around the perimeter that ran roughly ten feet apart and eight feet high with barbed wire strands every six inches, and was manned at all times by Japanese Guards.[2]

Among other things, Ruse remembers the remoteness of the camp, built a good distance from the city due to violent criminals that had historically been housed there: "Davao penal colony is right out in the middle of the jungle. It was the place where the Filipinos had sent convicts down who were up for long-term for crimes like murder.[a] In fact when we got there, there were still a few of the Filipino convicts there. There was two or three of them there and they had chains fastened to their ankles, and the other end had a big, heavy ball. They didn't stay long because they helped us as much as they could and the Japs didn't like that so they got rid of the rest of the Filipinos too," said Ruse.

As Dyess put it: "The only bright spot was the presence of our friends, the Filipino convicts. They were the grandest bunch of murderers and cutthroats I have ever known. They referred to us as 'the gentlemen prisoners.' They had been told by the Japanese authorities that if they taught the Americans to work hard, then they would receive pardons and walk out free, but as pardons never came, the convicts decided to make it as easy on their new friends as possible. 'They showed us how to appear very, very busy without actually doing anything.' It is amazing how little a Filipino can accomplish if he doesn't want to work. Yet you'd think he was going like sixty."[3]

Davao was still a productive place. Prisoners farmed various produce and also cut timber at a sawmill just east of the compounds. There was a hospital here that frequently had to treat the men who developed tropical ulcers from their work standing in one of nearly six hundred muddy rice paddies. The convicts at Davao had always raised their own food, and Ruse recalled that this was no different after their arrival: "The rice-paddies were out at a place called 'Mactan'. A little narrow-gauge railroad ran out to Mactan and every morning the rice-crew who were going to go out and work in the rice-paddies would load onto little flat cars on this narrow-gauge railroad and take their equipment with them and

---

[a] Dyess states that 80% of prisoners remaining at Davao had been incarcerated by the Philippine government for murder.

guards would go along. Mactan must have been six or seven miles out. Besides rice paddies, they had a pineapple plantation, they had fruit that just grew wild around there, but they wouldn't let us get any of it. Bananas, Papayas, and they even had a hog farm and a chicken farm."

Work in the Mactan rice paddies lasted year-round, with ongoing harvesting of different crops as they reached maturity. Prisoners working the Mactan detail did heavy long and hard work. If there were any benefit to this, it came in the chow line. Because of the heavy work involved, a larger serving utensil was used to dole out portions for the Mactan men. The special dipper was known as "the Mactan dipper". As a result of this practice, whenever anyone received a special favor in the camp, they referred to the act as "Getting a Mactan ration."[4]

"When we had been there a short time I noticed a chicken or hen in a little wire cage and a little sign in Japanese on the cage. I asked one of the guards (one of them that was very friendly and he could speak a little bit of English) what that chicken was doing in the cage. He said that she was caught eating her eggshells. I've heard that a chicken when it lacks protein it will eat the shells or anything like that. Anyway, she was being punished for eating her eggshells as if a chicken knew what she was locked up for. But this just gives you an idea of the mind of the Japanese," said Ruse.

"At Davao I plowed with a brahma bull that was assigned to me when plowing out in the dry land. I named him Bob. He had one horn that stuck straight up and the other one was down, and he was the meanest critter I've ever been around, boy was he contrary. They had a ring in their nose and about a fifteen foot chain fastened to that ring – a light chain, but heavy enough to hold a bull. On the opposite end of the chain there was a steal spike about sixteen to eighteen inches long that was sharpened on one end and had an eye on top, and the other end of the chain was fastened to that where we could stake him out. At night we'd drive that stake into the ground," said Ruse.

"This brahma of mine that they assigned me, I'd get up close to the front of him and he'd try and hook me when I'd go to hook him up to that plow in the morning when we'd start to work. He'd kick me eight times in the same spot before I could get out of the way. So, I was a little bit leery of him, but I finally figured out a way to hook him up without getting kicked," said Ruse.

Driven by starvation, the work on the farm provided ways for Ruse to supplement his diet. "We'd go over there to Mactan, and I think the first thing I plowed was corn. The corn stalks weren't very tall, but they were forming little ears. And we'd be plowing out there between those rows of corn and the Jap guards were on the perimeter of the corn fields. They wouldn't come in to where we were working; they'd stand out there and watch us. Being out there in that corn field, we could eat all the little tender corn cobs we wanted, and I filled up many a day on corn cobs. They're just about as good as grains of corn, but the little cobs had just formed. We'd grab one and shuck it real quick and when we got to a place where we knew the Japs couldn't see us we'd take a bite."

"We did the same thing in okra. We plowed okra, and I filled up a lot of days on raw okra. Another thing they raised over there they called camotes. It's like our sweet potatoes, and they taste a lot like sweet potatoes only they came in about three different colors. One was purple, one was yellow, and the other was white," said Ruse. "We were plowing those up, the camotes that had matured, and a crew would come along later and get 'em. When the Japs weren't looking we'd reach down real quick and grab one of those camotes. We wouldn't have time to peal it or anything, and we'd take a bite out of it."

"There's lots of ants over there in those fields and they had a hankering for camotes too," said Ruse. When you got one, of course you didn't have time to see if it was clean or anything, but if you picked up one that the ants had been eating on it was as bitter as quinine so we'd throw it away. There was a lot of days when I'd fill up on those camotes, or raw pumpkins, or young okra pods."

"We didn't get salt for our rice. They'd give us rock salt sort of like this salt we use to freeze ice cream in home freezers. The Japs would give us a handful of salt every evening after we got through work. We were supposed to hold our hand out and let the bulls lick it," said Ruse. "We'd all let them take maybe one lick. Then we'd throw the rest of it in our pocket. That's where we got what salt we had to put on our rice. We'd eat just anything to keep us going. I don't know if any Red Cross packages arrived for us, but we didn't get many of them. We received one package. The Japs took the rest."

"We had other sources of food like papayas, and bananas and things that grew wild around there. So for a while we could slip those into camp. One day I sneaked six big pineapples into camp. I had a blue denim jacket that was about a size forty-eight and I weighed about one-hundred pounds at that time (I later got down to eighty pounds at the time I was liberated, and when I enlisted I weighted one-hundred and forty)," said Ruse.

Each day the men made their way back to the guardhouse, and often would slip anything they could back into the camp as the guards were lax about searching for contraband. "I tucked those in my waistband and I stuck out all the way around like a pregnant woman only it was all the way around not just in front. The dumb Japs at the guard-house at the gate didn't have sense enough to know that I had something under my jacket," said Ruse.

"We would sneak things in like that and did pretty good as long as we could do that, but then one day one of the boys got careless and dropped a coconut or something like that at the guardhouse, at the guard's feet," said Ruse. "After that they started shaking us down when we went in there. The first day, that little guardhouse was stacked up clear to the ceiling with stuff we were slipping in."

"One day I snuck in a bunch of "kang kong". It looks like vines of ivy that people raise in pots in their house, and it tastes a lot like spinach if it's cooked. We could get things like that under our barracks which were up a few feet off of the ground and build a charcoal fire and cook," said Ruse.

"Well, one day ole Hubert Gregory, a boy in my outfit who lived in another barracks saw me with it and said 'Hey! Ruse! I worked over at the nip kitchen last night and I stole a bunch of pork broth. If you give me half of those greens, I'll give you half of my pork broth, and you'll have something that'll give them a little flavor when you cook.'" As it turns out, workers in the kitchen had befriended a small, white dog named "Lugao", whom Dyess described as being "a handful of white fur and a bag of bones", whom had been fattened up as much as possible by those who worked in the kitchen detail.

Figuring a little pork broth would be good, considering it was much more difficult to come by than the bland kang kong plants, Ruse made the trade. The next day Ruse found out that there had been no pork; Hubert and some of the boys in his barracks had cooked Lugao: "And that was dog broth that I had on my kang kong," said Ruse. "It didn't taste exactly like pork, but it did improve the greens a little bit."

Much of the food that the prisoners used to supplement their diet was found growing wild in the Philippine jungle. "There was one plant called a Cassava that looked considerably like a small willow tree. It grew up to about four or five feet tall and had leaves on it like a willow. You could dig one of those up and pull it up by the root, and it had a long root with bark on it. The root might be from one to two inches in diameter, and maybe about twelve to fourteen inches long. We'd take this bark off of the outside and it had a white meat in their like Irish potatoes. You had to split it down the middle because there was a long fibrous string down the middle that you had to take out of there. Then you could cook these; either boil them or bake them just about like you can Irish potatoes. In fact, I liked them better, I believe, than Irish potatoes. They were pretty good, and once in a while we'd get some of that and eat it," said Ruse.

The job of plowing in rice paddies had to been done in bare feet all while guiding the livestock that would pull the plow. It was the dirtiest and most physically taxing job at Davao. Occasionally, cobras and rice snakes could be spotted in and near the sunken rice-paddies. The only clothing was what the men called their "G-string" which consisted of a cloth about twelve inches wide and about thirty-six inches long with a sash affixed to one end. The cloth would be placed behind you, then brought up through the legs and tucked under the sash which was tied in front.[5] Despite all of the dangers and drawbacks, of the Mactan plowing details, the job became a source of nourishment in more than one way for Ruse. "To plow in the rice paddies we used these big ole grey looking beasts with flat horns that stick way out. Carabao, we called 'em."

"One day when we were plowing out there one of them got down in the mud in the rice paddy and couldn't get up and he died, so the Japs gave him to us to eat. Needless to say, after that, one got down and died pretty often, and they never did get wise to what was going on. We would do all kinds of plowing there with those Brahma bulls and with the Carabao[b]." According to Dyess, the men at Davao had a special recipe for cooking a Carabao: "You put a rock in the cooking pot with the meat and when the rock melts the carabao is tender."

II

A narrow-gauge railroad with a diesel engine carried men to work at Mactan while officers had the sought-after positions of doing maintenance work on the railroad. It became known to its riders as the "Toonerville Trolley," in tribute to the *Toonerville Folks* comic strip.[6]

"The railroad detail was made up of older, high-ranking officers, and their job was to go out with a Mactan train and work on the railroad," said Ruse. "They had little cars that could be hooked onto the tail end of a Mactan train. They'd take all of their tools and their water and everything. They'd get out to where they were going to work on the railroad and they would unhook from the train and the rest of them would go on to Mactan. Usually, they didn't have any guards along there with them, because it was right out there in the jungle, and they had no place to go."

"I had become acquainted with a major, Major Sheran from San Antone. He was on what they call a railroad detail. One evening Major Sheran, came up to me over where I was staying and said, 'Hey, how would you like to get on the railroad detail?' I said; 'I can't get onto that detail, because it's made up of officers.' He said, 'I think I can get you on it.' I said, 'I'm not even an officer,

---

[b] Before World War II, there were an estimated three million carabaos in the Philippines. By the end of the War it is estimated that nearly 70% of them had been lost.

Schmidt, L.S. (1982). American Involvement in the Filipino Resistance Movement on Mindanao During the Japanese Occupation. Thesis Presented to the US Army Command and General Staff College. Fort Leavenworth, Kansas. (P. 56).

and it's usually made up of *older* officers!' He said 'You can cook can't you?' I said 'Well, I can cook anything *we'd* have to cook.' Because the only way we could cook anything we would have was to throw it in a pot of water and boil it. So, he came back later and said that the Japs had agreed to let me go along as a Cook," said Ruse.

One morning, as the men were hooking the car to the Mactan train, Ruse went down to load his supplies onto the maintenance car at the end of the Mactan train, when Major Sheran approached him. "Major Sheran came over and asked me if I could cook a turkey. I said the only way we could cook it would be to boil it, and where are we going to get a turkey? He said 'We've got it. See that burlap bag on our car over there?' I said 'Yeah.' He said, 'There's a live turkey in there, a Filipino slipped it to me during the night.'

"So we got over there and we got ready to load up and board our flat car to go out to go to work. Usually they didn't send any guards along with us; they would all go with the Mactan bunch. But on this particular morning there was three guards that got on there, two young ones and one old sourpuss Sergeant. You could tell he hated Americans just by the way he'd look at us and would act," said Ruse.

"We got on the flat car and got ready to go and one of the little young guards saw that burlap bag and reached over and felt of it and it felt soft, so he sat down on it. And we all sat there on needles and pins all the way out," said Ruse.

The men had traveled out about four or five kilometers to the section of track where they were scheduled to work for the day, and unloaded their supplies and equipment. "We unhooked from our car and Major Sheran told the Jap Sergeant, that old sourpuss, that he was going to leave Captain George there with me to help me get the fire started and everything," said Ruse. "That seemed to be alright because he, the Jap, nodded, so we got off and got our cans of water to cook the rice in."

"We had a few camotes we were going to put in there with them, and we got the turkey and everything. The rest of them got on the car and went on down the track a ways to the place where they were going to work," said Ruse. "Captain George, incidentally, that's not his first name, it was his last name (I never did know his first name). I think it was "Lloyd" or something like that, but anyway, his last name was George."

"We had these cans they use over there in the Orient to put gasoline in, and that's what we cooked in and carried our water in," said Ruse. "We built a fire and skinned the turkey and cut him into halves. We had two five-gallon cans of water, and we put half of him in one can and half in the other, and we put some camotes in there and we started cooking the rice, and there was some cassava growing wild around there, so we got a few of those cassava roots, and skinned them and took the center out, and broke them up and put them in there too."

The working detail was stopped along the tracks next to an old Filipino shack, a nipa hut, just off of the tracks. "They build those things out of grass and bamboo, and the floors; they're built up off the ground maybe five or six feet off of the ground, maybe so the pigs can't get in. In this particular one, half of the flooring was gone. There was a big gap in the middle where the bamboo slats had come off of it or rotted off or something," said Ruse.

"When they came back from working on the railroad, these three guards came with them, and we all got up and got our food and got up in the hut to be in the shade to eat, and the Japs got on the other side of that hole in the floor, and we were on one side and they were on the other," said Ruse.

"They never did know we had turkey because it was cooked and we could just grab some meat off the bones and put it in with our rice. We got by with it and they never did know it, but I don't know how they kept from smelling it, because it sure didn't smell like rice," said Ruse.

"Anyway, during our lunch hour up there, one of these little guards looked at me and, of course I've had little guards like that all through the prison camps I was in, he asked me questions about where I lived. They started out in broken English, making signs, and if you'd act like you didn't understand what they were getting at, they would say, 'You're house-o. Where?', because they wanted to know where you lived. So, I told them where I lived, and they invariably, would look at you and shake their head and say, 'Oh, too bad, Japanese Skokie fly over," and he'd make a motion like an airplane falling over, and a motion like bombs falling, and say "Odessa *no more*." Or, wherever you told him you lived."

"So after this one asked me that and I answered him, I asked him where his house-o was, and he acted like he didn't understand what I was talking about," said Ruse. I said, '*Your house-o, where? Nagoya? Osaka? Tokyo? Where?*'"

"And when I did that dog-gone Sergeant jumped up and he carried one of those Samurai swords and he started swinging that at me and he was going to kill me! I could tell that that was his intention, but luckily with that gap in the floor he couldn't reach me," said Ruse.

"Major Sheran got up and sort of got in between us and calmed him down. We wondered all the way back in to camp what riled him up so much with me mentioning those Japanese cities. When we got into camp that night there was an old Navy Captain who had sneaked a small radio receiver in when we first went to Davao and he could get the news. This was along about that time when General Doolittle made his raid of Tokyo with B-25s, and we figured that that Sergeant thought that I was bragging when I was referring to and that I was laughing about that. He really came unglued," said Ruse.

Interactions such as these were commonplace between prisoners and their guards, but it did not take long for prisoners to take the comments with a grain of salt. One day, after only a short time in a camp, Dyess recalled a similar conversation with a prison guard in which he was being questioned by a Japanese guard that ended with an answer intended to instill fear, but ended up having the opposite effect. When the guard showed Dyess a map of the Pacific theater with Japanese flags drawn all over it, he displayed some visible consternation regarding the situation, and the guard responded by saying: "That not all." The guard grinned broadly. "Japanese submarines shell San Francisco, Japanese submarines shell Seattle. And, hah! Japanese submarines shell Chicago!"[7]

Not long after this incident, Ruse learned that some of his friends in the camp were being sent to Davao City on a work detail that would be building an airfield out of coral. "This one pilot in my outfit, Johnny McCown, from Grandview Texas, and James Nichols, he was a pilot in the 34th Pursuit Squadron; he lived in Ft.

Worth, and a Lieutenant Roy Russell who was a bomber pilot out
of the 28th Bomb Squadron, we were all pretty good friends and
we'd get together in the evening and talk a lot. About that time the
Japs decided to send a bunch down to Davao City to build an
airfield out of coral, and these fellows, these friends of mine were
all in the group selected to go down there. I tried to get to go and
the Japs wouldn't let me, so I have often wondered what ever
happened to them."

III

The Japanese guards wanted to make prisoners very aware
that attempts to escape were ineffective and perilous. An inner wall
patrol was recommended by the Japanese so that the officers could
save their own men from the consequences of futile attempts
desperation to get away. Even stepping too close to the perimeter
of the camp was enough to get a prisoner shot on the spot. One
day while Ruse was outside of the compound, he observed
firsthand the consequences of wandering too close to the perimeter.
"One of the boys was outside the compound there and he called to
a boy inside for something and this boy inside the compound went
over close to the fence. The Japs in the guard tower didn't know
what he was up to and they shot him and killed him."

At one time, three American Naval officers had escaped,
but had to turn themselves in only to protect the Filipino citizen
who had assisted them as the man and his family would have
potentially been executed.[8] The men were put to work at hard
labor and were given only rice and water to eat, and quickly became,
as Dyess described them, "living skeletons." Also in their attempts
to thwart subsequent escape attempts, another prisoner was put on
display to make an example and discourage other prisoners from
attempts to escape. "His feet were hobbled, his arms tied, and he
was lead around by a halter fastened about his neck. On his chest
was a sign that read: 'I tried to escape.' The guard that led him
around would say *These are three that try escape. You see, they come back
to us. You see what is becoming of them. You not should try escape.*'" The

day came when these three were no longer seen, and their demise was never doubted.[9]

Revenge against such acts was daydreamed about constantly, but was probably suicidal if attempted. One day, while on a work detail, a Filipino prisoner who had been flogged a few days earlier for selling leaf tobacco to an American found a chance for vengeance. When the Japanese guard sat down in the shade of a tree, he took his opportunity and buried an axe into the guard's neck. He then took a bolo and finished off the remains. After this, he took the guard's shoes and rifle and took to the jungle. Dyess remembered the aftermath as a satisfying event. "The Japs of Davao turned out en masse for an impressive funeral. After considerable ceremony, the dead man was placed upon a funeral pyre and burned. When the flames had died, the ashes were placed in an urn, and the Japs gathered up the beer, rice, meats, sweet cakes, and other foods that had stood near-by during the burning. These they removed to a small building so they would be ready at hand for the departed's spirit when he started his journey to the great beyond. Well, I guess that this was one Jap ghost that took his chow with him, because when they went back after it they found only empty beer bottles. It was the first beer I had in many a day. And with beef, too!"

Escape was a risk. Not only was it a personal risk, but it was a risk to the closest comrades of those who attempted it. As a result of previous escape attempts, one of the first orders of business upon arrival at Davao was to carry out a Japanese directive was produced that would group the prisoners in "shooting squads" of ten men. The command, dated July 10th, 1942, was to serve as a deterrent to escape and threatened that if any one prisoner escaped or attempted to escape, the remaining nine men would be executed.

Despite this new risk, escapes still were attempted, and still occasionally occurred. American leadership within the camp was forced to take preventative measures and forbade escape attempts; the risks involved were too great, not only for the escapees, but especially for those left behind. In order to enforce the ban on attempts at escape, POWs were stationed as patrols of the inner perimeter of the camp.

Davao

On Sunday, April 4th, 1943, ten men[c] escaped from Davao while out working on a detail. A Sunday was chosen because fewer men were sent out on details on Sundays, so guards would be relaxed. The men had been hoarding supplies in preparation for the escape as they were able to. They began taking food and supplies in preparation and spent several months scheming and planning their escape. Some of the men worked in an orchard picking coffee and various other fruit trees, which happened to be near the poultry farm. They would steal an occasional chicken and trade it for nonperishable food such as tinned fish or biscuits.

"The orchard detail wasn't too far out of camp so the Japs a lot of time wouldn't send a guard with them. We did not find out until later that these fellows had been planning this for a long time and had been stashing supplies to use in their getaway," said Ruse. "Finally, one day they told the Japs that they had a lot of work to do and they needed to get over there and finish something, so they let them go over there and work. Three of these fellows were in my outfit, the 21st Pursuit Squadron. Captain Dyess, he was one of the ring-leaders that escaped, and Lieutenant Sam Grashio, and Lieutenant Boelens", said Ruse.

Those that were preparing to escape were taking an incredible risk. Each time a new recruit was enlisted, they were more likely to be exposed, also, if their store of supplies were to be found, this put them at great risk as well. The escapees never told any of the other prisoners of their plans, most likely for their own protection, but also to keep control of their plans. Dyess was acutely aware of the risk: "If, after the escape the Japs should suspect any remaining prisoner of having advance knowledge of it, that individual's head would be as good as rolling in the sand," said Dyess. Several of the men in that detail were friends and fellow members of the 21st Pursuit Squadron with Ruse. Two of them were also members of his shooting squad.

While planning their escape, Dyess, Grashio and the other men had weighed the risks of retribution against their comrades left behind after their escape. They knew that if they were to harm any

---

[c] Two Filipino convicts still living at Davao also escaped at this time "Ben, and Victor" were useful because of their knowledge of the jungle.

guards during an escape would without question bring bloody reprisals upon remaining prisoners in the camp. A decision had to be made; No Japanese would be killed during the escape. Such an act could not be ignored, and vengeance would be certain.

The men planning the escape knew that Colonel Mori, the Commandant at Cabanatuan would have without doubt punished the escape of ten men with a large-scale murder of shooting squads. However, they felt that the Davao Camp Commandant, Major Maeda seemed more humane.

The men felt strongly that an escape, even with the great risks involved, was justifiable. Not just for their own personal freedom, but also because the world needed to know what horrors were taking place in Japanese prison camps. While the men all certainly recalled the fate of the three men who had been caught trying to attempt escape at Cabanatuan, according to Grashio; "...we eventually convinced ourselves that Major Maeda would not shoot nine or ten hostages for each of us who got away.[10]

"In the morning on the day of the planned escape, Sam Grashio came by. He and I and Hubert Gregory were pretty good friends. He came by and told Greg and I that they were going to go out and work on Sunday, they had some work they wanted to finish up, and he offered us a Jap cigarette. I told him no, I didn't want it. I hadn't had one in so long now I'm already accustomed to not smoking. I said, 'I'd rather you just keep it'. Sam said, 'You better take it, it may be a long time before I offer you another one'. At that time I thought nothing of it," said Ruse, "but that evening when I found out they had escaped, I knew that he meant he probably wouldn't be around to give me another one for a long time!"

Dyess, Grashio, and the other escapees had arranged to do voluntary work on Sundays, explaining to the guards that they would like to build a rain shelter near the coffee plantation so that they would have a place to go during downpours and would be less susceptible to colds. Major Maeda, pleased with the initiative that the men were taking, consented. Now, for the first time, the entire group of escapees would be able to leave the compound on Sundays without being questioned and without guards. The men could gradually build a stash of supplies in the jungle, and on the designated Sunday, check in for work as usual, then make their escape into the jungle with the hopes that no one would miss them until late in the afternoon. That late in the day, the Japanese may not even begin searching until the next morning, giving the men an entire day's head start.[11]

That evening at about 6:00 P.M., while the escapees were making their way through the jungle, Ruse found out that two of the men in his shooting squad had escaped while standing at attention during evening *tenko*, or roll-call. The men were called out and lined up, then counted as usual, then counted and recounted again. Each time, ten Americans and two Filipinos were unaccounted for.[12]

POW Manny Lawton, later recalled the speech that Major Maeda gave through his interpreter who was known to POWs as *Running Wada*:

> *"For every man who escape, de other nine in his squad wirr be shoot kirred. You are arr guilty of herping them escape. De major say you wirr arr be confined to camp untir he decide what what other punishment wirr be necessary."*[13]

Standing there in line at sunset, Ruse and the other men in the shooting squads had had no idea that the escape was to take place, which is a testament to the degree of secrecy that the escapees maintained; even with close friends. "They called us all out; about ninety of us, and took us over to another compound over about a kilometer from the main compound. They put us into a barracks there and told us that we'd have to stay there until Major Maeda flew to Manila to the Japanese High Command to find out what our punishment would be. They told us to stay inside till they found out what our punishment would be. They didn't know whether to go ahead and shoot us or what," said Ruse. Men from the squads were beaten and interrogated in an attempt to get information about the whereabouts of the escapees.

The next day, eighty five Japanese soldiers were sent out to search for the men, during their search they came across a group of ill-fated Filipinos who were shot.[14]

Back in the camp, the men were kept in the five thatch-roofed barracks, surrounded by three concentric barbed-wire fences for four days, uncertain as to what their fate would be. Meanwhile Maeda had to undertake the embarrassing task of reporting the matter to the Japanese Prisoner of War Bureau in Manila, under the command of Major General Ichiro Morimoto.[15]

The prisoners had seen the Japanese kill others when members of their shooting squads had escaped, but would they really kill ninety men? At Cabanatuan, the ten-man shooting squad rule was definitely in place, and no one had any reason to believe that there had been a change in that order. Some men resented the escapees for putting the lives of others at risk, while yet others admired their ability to pull it off. The next day as the men stood at attention the interpreter blasted the men with another of his infamous speeches: "Eleven American dogs have escaped from us. You must pay."[16]

The squads sat tensely in the camp with no news. Finally, on the fourth day, the men received word that Maeda had returned and the men would hear the reading of their sentence the next morning. That night was largely a sleepless one. The men stayed up and talked of many things, thinking that they could very well be executed the following morning. POW Bert Bank later recalled his thoughts: "We all wished that we would be given the same privilege that the men in the States are given before being executed, that of ordering anything they wished to eat. All night we said that this expected death would not be so bad if we could have some bread and butter and ham and eggs, and some cold sweet milk. In fact, there were many of us who would have given our lives for some food of this type."[17]

After the sleepless night, the men heard footsteps coming down the road at 8:45 A.M. Maeda was on his way, verdict in hand. Men working near the camp came to the fence with tears in their eyes to say final goodbyes: "Take it like men," they said. The men were "sacrificing our lives for other Americans, and that it was a wonderful way to die," recalled Bert Bank.[18]

Maeda entered the compound and the men were ordered to walk twenty paces to the front and stand at attention while Maeda read the sentence. Maeda and Wadda stepped onto a small box to address the crowd, and started by reading the names of each prisoner. "You will now hear your punishment," said Maeda through the interpreter as he unfolded a piece of paper from his pocket.

"Men called here due to insufficient control and supervision of their men, neglecting their duties, causing the escape of war prisoners, which is the *major* crime, have been giving the following punishments and are *directed to reflect their faults.* They shall thereby spend the number of days indicated in meditation of the past incident and observing modest and model conduct at all times," said Maeda.

"Major Maeda talked to us about thirty minutes in Japanese," said Ruse. "It took the interpreter about five minutes to tell us what he said. He said that the Jap High command in Manila had talked it over and they had formed the opinion that none of us knew that these other fellows planned to escape, so therefore we wouldn't be shot, however, we would be punished, and our punishment would be that we *wouldn't be allowed* to work for two weeks. We would have to stay in the barracks and meditate. And *boy*, we looked awful sorry. We all acted like we had just been whipped with a big stick. But, as soon as the Japs got out of there we had the biggest laugh we had ever had. Of course at that time most of us were working belly deep in mud out at the rice paddies, and we were really happy to get out of that for a time."

While this punishment seemed minor at the time, the entire camp was punished for the escape, not just those on the shooting squads, additionally; the tone of the camp had become more harsh for the prisoners. Guards became much more cruel in their dealings with the men on working details, and beatings became more frequent and severe. Additionally, for a period of time, rations were cut for the entire camp.[19] Yet, for the time being, the men were happy to make it with their lives. As their friends went out to toil in the sun for their working details, Bert Bank would badger the men on their way out: "The other fellows would go to work in the rice fields and I would tell them not to bother me that *I was meditating.* You just can't figure out these people."[20]

The men who had escaped would for years ahead have to rationalize what they had done with themselves while knowing that they had put others in danger. Grashio would later say that having not known how the men left behind felt about the escape would weigh heavily on his conscience, until crossing paths with them many years later and learning of what had actually occurred.[21]

In Ruse' case, Grashio was correct in his assumption that there had been no bitter resentment towards those who had escaped. Although, it might have been understandable for those left behind to harbor anger at those who had escaped, because their lives had legitimately been put in danger, this was not the case. The men who remained at Davao were already uncertain of their own survival on a day to day basis, and had hopes that an escapee would get word back to the states and spread the word about the treatment that prisoners of the Japanese had received in the Philippines. This ultimately, was a large part of the legacy of Ed Dyess. Ruse would tell the story of his friends' escape with pride, and pleasure that it had earned him a break from plowing in a muddy swamp via a punishing two weeks of meditation!

Nevertheless, the escapees for the remaining duration of the war had to live with questions as to what happened to those left behind at Davao. After working with Filipino guerilla fighters and managing to evade the Japanese on Mindanao, Sam Grashio finally was able to board a U.S. submarine, the *USS Bowfin*, bound for Australia, a truly liberated man. Boarding the ship, Grashio had contradictory emotions; he was thrilled at the prospect of going home, and of telling the Americans of the horrors that were still taking place in the prison camps, but at the same time could not forget his friends still in the camp at Davao. "I could never put out of my mind memories of my fellow prisoners back in Davao. What were they enduring now because ten of us had escaped? The thought bedeviled me constantly."[22]

Grashio soon returned to the U.S., where he was debriefed at the Pentagon and informed that he could not speak about his experiences as a POW. Even as he received "scores of letters and phone calls" from family members of POWs immediately after his return, Grashio was under legitimate orders not to speak of that which he knew. At the Pentagon, his directives were made clear:

> "...State Department functionaries merely told me in a patronizing way what I was and was not allowed to do. To them, no doubt, it appeared that I had a fixation about prisoners and that I had lost sight of the War as a whole. To me, they seemed unreasonable, even inhuman; preoccupied with Europe when American soldiers were starving, rotting, and dying in squalid

prison camps; far too concerned about the reactions of Japanese and too little about the fate of Americans abroad and the anxieties of their loved ones at home."[23]

With no outlet for the information that he and the other escapees held, and yet carrying the burden of the POWs that remained in the Philippines, understandably, this was a very frustrating, and irritable time for Grashio.[24]

Grashio was not the only one who had been "muzzled." It would be January of 1944 before the story of the imprisonment and escape would finally appear to the public as *The Dyess Story* in the *Chicago Tribune*, which would have an audience of twelve to fourteen million readers. Dyess had made it back to the states on August 9th his twenty-seventh birthday, and had given a lengthy set of interviews both to government officials and to a *Tribune* writer, but the interviews had not been immediately released for publication. By February, an account was printed in *LIFE* magazine. The combination of these accounts infuriated the public, demanding swift revenge on behalf of those held captive.[25]

Revenge was a priority secondary to survival for Carl Ruse. In Davao, and all over the Pacific theater, the surviving prisoners battled on.

That September, Ruse managed to let his family know that he was alive and well after over two and a half years in captivity. The postcard had been pre-filled with no room for writing details with the option to fill-in-the-blanks for the recipient. As he scratched his name on the card, Ruse knew that anything he wrote was subject to Japanese censorship. He just wanted to get word home that he was actually alive.

With the possibility of censorship in mind, prisoners often would attempt to communicate through codes or even bible verses. A reference to Second Corinthians, Chapter one, verse eight was frequently penned:

"For we do not want you to be unaware, brethren, of our affliction which came to us in Asia, that we were burdened excessively, beyond our strength, so that we despaired even of life."[26]

When E.D. Ruse retrieved his mail that third week of September, 1943, he found a postcard stamped with American and Japanese Postmarks. With overwhelming relief he read the following lines:

IMPERIAL JAPANESE ARMY

1. I am interned at: <u>the Philippine Military Prison Camp No. 2.</u>

2. My health is- excellent; good; <u>fair;</u> poor.

3. I am - injured; sick in hospital; under treatment; <u>not under treatment.</u>

4. I am - improving; not improving; better; <u>well.</u>

5. Please see that_____ is taken care of.

6. (Re: Family); <u>Please see that everyone who might care knows that I am alright.</u>

7. Please give my best regards to; <u>everyone.</u>

IV

Davao POW Russell Hutchinson had managed to build a secret radio out of smuggled parts, and became the sole source of reliable news in the camp. He kept the set disassembled during the day and managed to assemble and monitor it at night while friends stood guard. In May of 1944, Hutchison heard of an American Naval victory near the Palau Islands; only a few hundred miles from Mindanao. The prisoners noticed that the Japanese began winding the camp down to a close. Work in the rice paddies was slowing, and vegetable gardens weren't being replanted as regularly.[27]

The fight was coming back to the Philippines. By the nineteenth of June, unbeknownst to the POWs, the Battle of the Philippine Sea was underway. The Japanese Navy was suffering heavy losses; particularly that of irreplaceable trained air crews. In a sweeping change of hats, it was now the Japanese who were on the run. But, time would tell that this was not immediately a positive change in fortune for the surviving prisoners still remaining on the islands. As allied advances in the Pacific progressed, Japan began efforts to move their prisoners back to their mainland. It was late June of 1944. The Philippine islands were only months away from liberation, yet, the POWs were being moved yet again, and this time to the home of the enemy. [28]

"We were put on trucks and went to Davao City, and put on one of these ole' Jap 'Hell-ships,' as they were later called, to go back to Manila," said Ruse. "I have no idea how long we were on that ship, some of them seem to think we were on there about two weeks on that ship going back to Manila, but I don't have any idea. I never did try to keep track of time because it didn't matter so much then. All I thought about was getting out of there one of these days."

The trip to Manila in the hold of a ship was only glimpse of what awaited the prisoners who would survive long enough to be taken to Japan. From the time the group would leave Davao, ninety-two days would be spent in traveling to their final destination.

At Bilibid, the men were held in a large, open yard on the prison grounds that had been badly damaged from bombing and shelling early in the war. There was no cover overhead, so time spent at Bilibid was spent exposed to the elements. There were several spigots of water, but the water was only turned on for short periods of time.[29]

When Ruse arrived in Manila, he was placed in Bilibid Prison[d] for three days. "We learned that the able-bodied men were going to be shipped on to Japan and I was one of the able-bodied ones I guess, even though I had lost so much weight, I was still one of the able-bodied ones. Just before we got ready to leave Bilibid to go get on the ship for Japan, Frank Harangody out of my outfit, who had lost one leg on Bataan, came in to where I was and said, 'Have you got any personal items you'd like to keep?' He said the Japs were taking all of those personal items away from us."

---

[d] Bilibid Prison was a former civilian prison converted to a POW camp, hospital and transit camp for POWs. It was a transit point for movement to other camps, e.g., Davao, and for hell ships to Japan, so many survivors of Bataan passed through at least one point during time as POWs. Retrieved from
http://www.mansell.com/pow_resources/camplists/philippines/bilibid/bilibid_main.htm
l on 2/15/2010.

"They had let some mail get through to us, and I had two or three postcards from my Dad, and I wanted to keep them. Harangody said "If you do have, it might be a good idea to leave them with me." He said 'I know I'm not going to Japan, they don't want anyone there that can't work.' He said 'When we get back to the states I'll send it to you.' So I gave him everything that I had, and we went down to the dock and were loaded on another hell-ship to go to Japan, and we set out into the Manila Bay in the hold of this ship, crowded in there like sardines. Later, Frank kept his word and I got a letter and he sent me the things that I had given him there."

It was at Bilibid where more goodbyes were in store for the men who had been on Mindanao at Davao Penal Colony. The group would be splintered from this point forward, some were taken to other camps, and others were going to Japan. Some would survive the journey, and many would not make it; either dying en route from the conditions aboard the ships, or being killed as the transport ships they rode in were torpedoed.

CHAPTER IX

THE HELL SHIP

What vision of Hell can compete with the realities we now confront?

C. Wright Mills

The Bible says that Hell is low and hot; there is no escape. It is a place "where the fire never goes out." A place of deep sorrow where the stench of death is in the air; a place in the control of evil. It is a place that is absent from God.

Week after week—through violent typhoons and dreadful heat—prisoners of war were kept in the below-deck hold of the *Canadian Inventor*. The only word that came to mind in the place was "hell." They could think of no better word to describe a place on earth. It was a place of no freedom, of only endurance and suffering or death. It was low. It was hot, and it was dirty. The dry misery of the hot air would settle into the tongue and make a man gag. It was a place of every imaginable physical suffering in addition to being yet another display of the evil cruelties that

We Volunteered

mankind is capable of when its cultures lose regard for human life. Hell is a place of a sort of misery that exceeds human understanding, and perhaps in an attempt to imagine it, the mind takes us to the most awful physical and mental torment that might be imagined. In the mind's eye this becomes a vision of hell. The hold of a crowded, dark, hot, and putrid-smelling ship brought a vision of hell from a place in the mind's eye to an actual place on earth; a man could just not imagine a place any worse. *This* was hell, and the POWs who were there could think of no better adjective to describe it.

Carl Ruse left his friend Frank Harangody at Bilibid Prison on July 2nd, 1944. The men marched to Pier Seven and lined up to board the rusty and neglected old ship floating high in the Manila Bay. They were in a different world than they had seen only two and a half years earlier when they had walked down the platform from the *President Coolidge*. This was far from a luxury liner.

Despite all they had been through, having to leave the Philippines was an exceptionally bitter pill to swallow. The men had heard that the Allies were advancing, that the war was coming to an end, and that they might even be home soon. Now, the enemy was retreating, and after all they had survived, they were being taken away at the end of it all.

The two holds of the *Canadian Inventor* were crowded with other POWs. The old boat had been taken from Canada while in Singapore, and was converted by the Japanese to use as a freighter for their war efforts. The smell of hay and manure met them as they arrived on the deck, and climbed through the hatch to a stale, and dark sardine can where temperatures could reach 130° in the tropical climate and equatorial latitude.[1] After boarding, the men sat for two days before the ship attempted to depart. The hold of the ship was about twelve feet deep and packed so tight that the only way all of the men could sit at the same time was with their knees drawn up to their chests. There was no room to lie down and stretch out unless someone was to make room for another man by standing up.[2]

The ship finally set sail on July 4th, but had to return in less than twenty-four hours due to boiler trouble. The ship finally set sail again on July 16th. The men had already been in the ship for

118

two weeks, and were finally making actual progress toward a destination. The stench in the ship was horrible, as there were no latrines, only buckets on the floor that were always full. "All of this time we were in there in that hold in weather that was over a hundred degrees," said Ruse. "Finally we got started again after we got that boiler repaired or replaced, but we were stopped several times en route to Japan."

Soon after leaving Manila, the seas became rough, tossing the ship and its passengers with each wave. Carl Ruse took bets with the men in the hold about whether or not the next wave would be the last one the old rusty ship could take: "During that time we passed through the typhoon we did a lot of betting on the waves. The boat would rock over where the deck would be straight up and down and some of the fellows would bet, the next time it's going to roll completely over. Others would bet it wouldn't, but it would finally rock back every time. That was the roughest water I was ever in. We were lucky to pull through it in that old Jap boat." The waves would rock the boat so violently that men would slide over the lower decks with nothing to hang on to; the skin of their hides with bones protruding just below the surface becoming raw from sliding back-and-forth over the rough-hewn planks of the lower deck.

"We stopped at Formosa,[a] where we took on a load of salt, rock salt like we use ice-cream freezers in the states. They loaded the hold of the ship we were in with rock-salt and the rest of the way to Japan we had to sit on that salt, but we didn't mind that because on the way to Japan with what little rice we got, we'd at least have some salt to put on it," said Ruse.

"I don't know how long we were at Formosa, but we were there several days, and we had to sit on the salt all of the way to the rest of the way to Japan," said Ruse. While stopped, the Japanese captors took the men on the deck and sprayed them down with fire hoses, before having to go back under the deck. Day after day they sat in the hold, the ship not moving. The men had been in the boat for over one month; finally setting sail again on August 4th, but after

---

[a] The Canadian Inventor made this stop in the Taiwan City of Takao (Kaohsiung) on July 23rd, 1944, and finally set sail in August 4th.

only a few hours of sailing more boiler trouble sent the ship to shore again at Keelung, a port city in northeastern Taiwan. It would be twelve more days sitting in the hold of the ship before they would move again.

"Sometimes there was an American Submarine in the water in the vicinity and they would hug the shore of those islands so they couldn't be detected as easily," said Ruse. "I don't know how many altogether of those hell-ships they had that they shipped fellows to Japan in, but ours was at sea sixty three days for some reason. I don't know why it took so long, but we were there sixty three days in the hold of that ship and about the only thing we had to relieve ourselves was a five-gallon bucket that they lowered down to us. The whole time people were dying from dysentery and other things."

The five-gallon buckets used as latrines were quickly filled to overflowing and were quickly of no use. Men who were healthy enough might be allowed to go on deck to relieve themselves. However, since intake of food was so low, their output was limited as well. To get to the hatch, a man would weave through the crowd and ask permission to climb up the ladder to go to the *benjo* on the decks. Since only four could be on deck at a time, there was always a line. The deck-level latrines consisted of four boxes that attached to the ship outboard of the rails. The boxes were about three feet square and two feet deep, and had a large opening in the floor. To use the box, one had to step inside and place his feet on the ledges to keep from falling through. If using the latrine during the high seas of the typhoon, men had to hang on tight during the violent rocking of the ship. Ray Heimbuch, a POW on the ship said the following of using the latrine during the typhoon; "The roll of the ship would cause you to be twenty-five or thirty feet above the water at the high point of the roll, and awash in the sea at the low point."[3]

Cleanliness was impossible in the filthy condition. When it rained, the first thought the men had was to catch as much water as possible to drink, and then to wash off as much grime as possible while the rain fell. During the entire time on the ship, men could not change, or even take off the clothes on their backs for three months.[4]

120

II

The *Canadian Inventor*, with the exception of its extraordinarily long travel time, actually fared well compared to many ships that departed for the Philippines. Between 1942 and 1945, twenty one thousand prisoners of war died en route or went down with sunken ships.[5] "As it turns out, we were very, very lucky that we got on that one because not long after that, the boys that came out of the Philippines were torpedoed or bombed by American bombers because the Japs did not mark them in any way and our people didn't know that they were carrying prisoners."

"In fact I found out later that these friends of mine who had left Davao to go down and help build the airfield were on one of these ships and it was torpedoed by an American submarine. I believe out of the twelve to fourteen-hundred men on board, there was eighty survivors, and Roy Russell, one of these friends of mine, he was the only one out of this bunch of friends of mine that survived. Since then he has been by to see me since we've gotten back."

"He said that he and the other fellows were in the hold of this freighter and this torpedo hit. The next thing he knew, he came to out in the water and looked around and the Japs were going around in life boats killing the boys in the water with swords or shooting them, so he kept ducking under," said Ruse.

"The ship had been hugging the shoreline because they were afraid of American submarines and he kept ducking under and swimming under water and he finally made it to shore and a Filipino guerilla found him there and took him over to there camp. They had contact with Australia and they sent a submarine from Australia to pick him up, but he had a pretty rough time. I think nearly every hell-ship after that was torpedoed or bombed for no reason at all; if they had just marked them that there were prisoners there it wouldn't have happened," said Ruse.

III

The passage from Manila to Moji, the primary port of entry for POWs into Japan was 1,276 nautical miles, and could, under normal conditions, make the passage in fifteen days. But under wartime conditions, with allied air patrols and submarines patrolling, the days in the hold of the Canadian Inventor kept adding up. The men renamed the ship *Matte-Matte Maru*, "the Waiting-Waiting Ship".[6]

After ninety-two days of travel, on September 2nd 1944, the POW's disembarked the *Canadian Inventor* in the port city of Moji, Japan, leaving one cavern of hell for another. [b]

---

[b] The entire trip from Davao to Moji took 92 days, including time spent at Bilibid Prison - Interview with Raymond C. Heimbuch, former POW. The journey from Bilibid to Moji was 63 days. Retrieved from URL http://www.us-japandialogueonpows.org/Heimubuch.htm on 4-3-2010.

The Hell Ship

"Canadian Inventor" Hell ship. Also known as the "Matte-Matte Maru" (Waiting-Waiting Ship), or "Canadian Maru".

Aerial photograph of the Yokkaichi beach and prison camp. Note the long warehouse building with the letters "PW", on the roof, identifying the as housing for prisoners of war. Also note the smokestack at right. Courtesy of Bill Briggs, of the *HMS Indefatigable.*

CHAPTER X

YOKKAICHI

He who has a *why* to live can bear with almost any *how*.

-Friedrich Nietzsche

By the time of the POW arrival in Japan, the Japanese hopes of victory were diminished. Prisoners were being moved from the Philippines to Japan, and many died during the journey there. In July of 1945, Japanese diplomats were being forced to consider peace negotiations through Moscow. Defeat was not known in Japanese history nor did it exist in the vocabulary of the Japanese conscience, but at this point their defeat was unavoidable. The Japanese government had started a war, without believing it could defeat the United States, only hoping to negotiate a peace on favorable terms, being left to their old order, and with a military-driven government still in power. But now, as resources were quickly being depleted, this was no longer an option either. American victories were spreading across the Pacific Islands, and the Japanese knew that a decisive battle was going to occur, and would likely occur on the beaches of the main islands of the homeland. A paper was in circulation in the offices of the Army and Navy General staffs. Called "Ketsu-Go", this was the Japanese last effort for the final battle that would decide the outcome of the war.

The plan would call for the final employment of every available weapon and resource the Japanese had. Thousands of aircraft had been prepared for use as suicide planes; hidden under trees or camouflage, with only enough fuel in the tanks for one trip to a beach being invaded. Return was not part of the strategy. Runways were narrow swaths cut through grassy meadows. They could only afford a single battle, and it must not pass the beach, so every resource would be spent there. The plan was to kill as many Americans as possible and crush morale. Civilians would fight along soldiers with bamboo spears, and were encouraged to commit suicide before being captured.[1]

As a POW, Ruse had heard of Ketsu-Go: "We found out that their plan was to try to have all of the POWs in Japan, and as the Americans got too close to their homeland, and made landing on Japanese soil, we would all be done away with. In fact, they had already issued orders to that effect. I'll never, ever forget old Harry Truman for sending those bombs over and putting a stop to it because that's what got us back home. I think a heck of a lot of Harry Truman and his atomic bomb. If it hadn't been for that, well, we would have never got out of there."

After all that the POWs had survived thus far, the plan was to kill them all in the event of an invasion. This was the hopeless world into which the surviving POWs entered in 1944. The war could not be sustained much longer. Some sort of a violent end was inevitably coming, and it would be coming soon.

Sure enough, plans for extermination of POWs materialized when Japanese soldiers massacred close to 150 inmates at the Palawan POW Camp. As allied troops advanced on the islands, the men were ordered into bomb shelters underground which they had built themselves for their own protection. After the men were safely inside, gasoline was poured on the death trap and ignited with torches. As the men attempted to escape, many were shot, bayoneted, or met hand grenades. In the end, only eleven men managed to escape. The Ketsu-Go plan was more than just a plan; at Palawan in December of 1944, it was a reality.[2]

Yokkaichi

On April 12th of 1945, President Roosevelt was posing for an artist who was producing a watercolor portrait of the President. While being served lunch, President Roosevelt complained of a "terrific" pain in his head, and subsequently collapsed. He died that afternoon from a cerebral hemorrhage.

Less than a month later, Allied forces formally accepted the unconditional surrender of Nazi Germany; victory in Europe had come at last. President Truman had been Commander-in-Chief for only twenty-six days. His family had moved into the White House and slept there for the first time just the night before.[3]

II

While the Ketsu-Go document circulated in Japan, on the 28th of May, 1945, another document was also circulating that outlined a plan for Allied invasion of Japan. The cover of the document was simply titled: "*Operation Downfall: Strategic Plan for Operations in the Japanese Archipelago.*" Downfall was a set of directives intended to force Japan into unconditional surrender. As Japan suspected, the plan did call for the "invading and seizing objectives in the industrial part of JAPAN."

The Japanese had been correct in anticipating an invasion of their homeland. The plan called for the invasion of Kyushu, then Honshu. As it turns out, the Japanese had appropriately guessed that these beaches would be invaded first and defense strategists began assembling troops there. However, an omission had been left out of the American plan, and of course, the Ketsu-Go plan of the Imperial Army.

When the Imperial Army had taken an inventory estimating the whereabouts of the United States Army and Navy forces, a May 8 notation appending the list of B-29 squadrons still believed to be in the United States read: "One other unit is available but its identity has not been ascertained yet." The missing Squadron was the 393rd Bombardment Squadron, which was presently preparing to leave the United States for its new home on the island of Tinian, in the Mariana island chain. The 393rd was part of the 509th Composite

Group; Its mission was to drop atomic bombs on the cities of Japan.[4]

III

It had been sixty three days when the hell-ship landed in Japan in the port city of Moji. Ruse walked out of the filthy, hot, crowded ship, yet again managing to survive when many had not.

Disembarking the ship, any sense of relief to be out of the ship was short lived, given the reception that the men received. The first steps he took on land in nine weeks were met with torment at the hands of Japanese civilians: "We arrived in Moji and were marched down through the basement of a railroad station. Civilians were lined up in two lines facing each other. We had to walk between them, and they spit on us and hit us as we went through to the other end of the station," said Ruse.

The men were marched to a set of abandoned stables near the train station that was filled with straw that had been used for horses and were given a boxed-lunch, and had water available to attempt to get cleaned up. The men spent two days in the stables at Yokkaichi, receiving two boxed-lunches per day, consisting of rice, a vegetable, and a pickled radish, which was a welcome addition from the rations on board the ship.[5] The next day the men boarded a train and left Moji.

"We boarded the train and they took us over to a place called Yokkaichi.[a] The prisoners traveled northeast from Moji by train up the Japanese archipelago via Hiroshima, Kobe, and Osaka to their ultimate destination in the industrial city of Yokkaichi.

"Yokkaichi was the first and only prison camp I was a prisoner in while in Japan," said Ruse. "We were there exactly one

---

[a] Yokkaichi, Japan is approximately 250-300 miles from Moji, Japan. Most prisoners here arrived via the Canadian Inventor and Nissyo Maru Hellships. Primary purpose was sulphuric acid manufacturing.
http://www.mansell.com/pow_resources/camplists/Nagoya/nag_5_yokkaichi/nag_05_yokkaichi_main.html Retrieved 2-15-2010.

year." The prison camp at Yokkaichi consisted of several long, barn-like, floorless barracks on a sandy beach that housed about one hundred fifty men.

The men had left Davao on June 6th, 1944; it was now September 5th. The transports left the sweltering heat in Manila and arrived to a shocking cold, sometimes at zero degrees and below with snow and sleet. In Northern Asia, the winter was one of the coldest in decades. Upon his arrival, the forced labor continued for Ruse, and approximately six-hundred fifty other prisoners at Yokkaichi. "The prison compound was a dark, dismal place with a ten or twelve foot black fence around it," said Ruse. Each barracks had a center aisle about ten feet wide with a fire pit built into the ground, however, the only fuel furnished was a small amount of charcoal each day. The men would attempt to steal and carry in small scraps of wood each day, but this was hardly enough to heat the large and drafty barracks built right on the sand of the beach. The men were issued two blankets each, and slept on a raised platform that ran the length of the barracks on each side of the aisle, and slept on straw mats that were about an inch thick. Meals at Yokkaichi consisted of a mixture of rice and barley, and a soup made from radishes. [6]

"We were sent to work over at a factory, they called it, but to me it was more like a smelter.[b] They had blast-furnaces and they took all of these items made out of copper and brass that they had taken from the islands that they had took over, and brought them in to melt up and use in their war efforts. The copper smelter was about a thousand yards from our compound."

"There was a mound of these items outside of the factory there nearly as big as a rodeo coliseum. Women would bring them in there, carrying them in baskets. These women would work in there with babies strapped onto their backs, and they'd carry those items like cigarette lighters, cigarette holders, idols, lamps, and things like that, made out of brass or copper. They would bring them in there and dump them in to be melted."

---

[b] This company was probably the Ishihara Sangyo Company. This company along with multi-billion dollar companies as Mitsubishi Corp., Mitsui & Co. Ltd., and Nippon Steel Co. greatly benefited due to the slave labor of POWs during World War II.

This young Japanese boy was befriended by Ruse while working in the factory Yokkaichi, and would sneak food to him when possible. After liberation, Ruse left a great deal of food with the boy and his family. The boy gave him this photograph. Ruse never knew his name. See the afterword for more on the search for "the boy."

Yokkaichi

"While I was working there, there was an old Japanese man and a little Japanese boy that I figure was about ten years old, and he would slip food to me every once in a while. The boy and I became pretty good friends, although he couldn't show it. He would slip food to me although he really couldn't spare it. Food was very scarce, even for the Japs. I never knew his name."

"When we first landed in Yokkaichi they took pictures of us, and gave each of us a number. I guess this was as a means of identification in case any of us managed to escape, but in Japan, there's no place to escape to because you would be easily detected. I'm sure we'd probably the only ones in the vicinity that didn't have slant-eyes. My number was five-hundred and fifty. *'Go-yaka-goju'* in Japanese. In Japanese, it's easy to learn to count. You say *'iti, ni, san, si, go, roku, siti, hati, ku, zyuu'*, then you get to ten then you start over and you say 'ten-one, ten-two, ten-three, ten-four, ten-five, ten-six', and you get to twenty and you'd say *'ni'*. Ni is for two. You'd say 'two-one, two-two, two-three, two-four' and on up. So, it was real easy to learn to count off in Japanese, and we'd have to 'fall in' in the morning and we'd have to count off in Japanese, and they'd give us orders in Japanese and march to work, and we'd get over in front of this big smokestack. For some reason they worshipped that smokestack. Also, the rising sun, I always heard they worshipped the rising sun, but we would have to stop in front of that smokestack, and they'd give us orders to left face so we'd be facing the smokestack. *'Migi muku migi!'* was left face. Then they'd say *'Dasabo!'*, that's hats off. Then we'd take our hats off. We had to wear one of these old silly Japanese caps. Then they'd say *'Chakabo'*, hat's on then. Then *'Migi nari!'* is right face, and we'd start out again to the plant, but we did that every morning. Every time we passed by that smokestack we'd have to stop and bow to it, and I never did know what the reason was for it."

The men at Yokkaichi worked in several different details in the immediate area of the camp. "I worked at a place called *'Shokets'*-I never did know what *Shokets* meant, but anyway, our job was to furnish the fuel for these blast furnaces[c]. They had a big,

---

[c] In Japanese, the word "Shouketsu" (焼結) means to sinter, or to make ore into a mass of metal by heating it yet without melting it. Thank you to Wes Injerd for advising on this translation.

long conveyor belt that ran into this machine and there were chemicals on both sides of the conveyor belt and there were men on both sides of the belt shoveling these chemicals onto the conveyor belt. They would go into the machine and the machine would grunt and groan and make up that stuff, whatever it was, then it would come out the other side in a log-like roll about four inches in diameter, and we would break those off in about eight-inch lengths and load them into a little car on a narrow-gauge railroad." The men had a nickname for the grunting and groaning machine that they worked with, however, Ruse chose not to repeat the moniker that the men used for the dirty, and shuddering old contraption after they had returned to civilized society, saying "I won't say what we called the machine we worked with!"

"We loaded the fuel onto the railroad when it came out of the machine and when we would get the car full we would push it over and dump it into the blast furnace," said Ruse. I don't know what it was, but it sure did make a hot fire. That was the only place I worked during the year I was in Japan."

When he first entered the camp at Yokkaichi, Ruse was taken aback by the cultural differences in the highly industrialized city. To him, it seemed that the Japanese at the time "were a hundred years behind us."

"Just to give you an idea how backward the Japs were in those days, there was an old Japanese woman and a boy that looked like he was about maybe ten years old building a smokestack," said Ruse. "This old Japanese woman and this boy building a smokestack, they'd build a form up a short ways, and they had a scaffold there. They had a wheelbarrow and they'd mix concrete in, and this old woman would get down off of this scaffold and have this boy mix concrete, and she'd get back on there. He'd shovel the bucket (about a five-gallon bucket full of concrete), and she'd lift it up and dump it in the forms. When they got the cement up to the top of the form they would build a form on up higher; I guess the smokestack was about twenty five or thirty feet tall when they finished it. Incidentally, when we were coming out exactly one year later, they had just finished the smokestack."

"We passed most of our time with, it was our indoor-sport, I guess you could call it, mashing fleas between our thumbnails. We had fleas all over us-sand fleas as we were out on this beach. In the Philippines, we'd had bedbugs and lice. We never did have both of them at the same time," said Ruse. I never did figure out whether the lice ate the bedbugs, or the bedbugs ate the lice, but we never did have both at the same time, but we always had some kind of bug. In Japan we had the fleas, and there was no way to get rid of them. They'd get in the waistband of your trousers and we'd pick 'em out of there and mash 'em between our thumbnails."

For the smokers in the camp who had managed to maintain the practice after years as a prisoner, Ruse observed another popular sport: "The Jap guards would give the boys a cigarette for each rat they caught and gave them."

IV

On the afternoon of December 7th of 1944 Ruse was working in the smelter as usual when the violent tremors of the *Tonankai* Earthquake hit Japan. The magnitude 8.1 quake destroyed or heavily damaged more than seventy three thousand houses in Japan from Honshu (over one hundred miles to the north), to the island of Kyushu, over two hundred miles to the south. "At the time of the earthquake I was working near a concrete wall. This wall gave way and fell on my foot and broke my foot," said Ruse. "I had always read about earthquakes where the ground would crack open and water will shoot up in your face. This was the case here in this one," said Ruse. "The ground would crack open and water would shoot up out of the ground and we wouldn't know which way to step to get away from things like that. In other words, about the time you step one direction, the ground was liable to crack open."

"Over toward the factory where we worked there was a smokestack. We had heard that it was the tallest smokestack in the orient. I guess it was about three or four-hundred feet tall or a little taller, and had a diameter about twenty or thirty feet thick at the base. During this earthquake, I got to watching that thing, and I knew there was a bunch of boys working around the base of it. It was just rocking back and forth, and finally about twenty feet broke off and just scattered around the base, and I thought, 'Boy! There's gonna be a lot of fellows killed,'" said Ruse. "But evidently they all got out of the way because there was only one other person that got hurt during the quake besides me and that was a Mexican boy named Jose Loya from San Benito Texas."

"Loya was working up in the building over there at the factory up on the second floor, and he got scared and jumped out the window and broke his leg. If he'd stayed there he'd have been alright, but he got his leg broke. He and I got to be pretty good friends because we were the only ones in the group that were injured in that earthquake," said Ruse.

That night after the earthquake, a tidal wave rolled in through the bay, hitting the barracks with six feet of ocean water. The bays where the prisoners slept had lower and an upper levels, which allowed for them to have a place to escape to as the wall of water swept through. "The upper bay was up about ten feet, and we all got up in there and we had to stay up there until the water went down," said Ruse.

In the southern Island of Honshu, on the east coast peninsula of Kii, tidal waves reached a height of twenty six feet in a wall of water that washed away another three thousand houses. The wave rolled as far as Alaska, where a small wave was detected.[d]

"After the earthquake, I had to work five days with a broken foot before the boys finally convinced the Japs that I had a broken foot and to let me stay in," said Ruse. "They finally convinced the Jap Corporal who was in charge of the little old make-shift hospital they had there, that I had a broken foot. They got him to feel the bones drift together, and past each other. So he let me stay in. Cecil Crouch, a fellow from Chandler, Oklahoma, was a medical corpsman in the U.S. Army, he made me a pair of crutches out of a two-by-four. He split a two-by-four down the middle and took each half and split it part way down, then spread

---

[d] The 1944 Tonankai Earthquake as described at the website for the United States Geological Survey.
http://earthquake.usgs.gov/earthquakes/world/events/1944_12_07.php (retrieved 6-7-2010)

the two parts out and fastened them together where I could put my arms over, and that's how I got around."

"In the camp at Yokkaichi, we had a latrine that we would get up and use at night at the barracks where we stayed. We'd have to go back there to go to the bathroom, or to go back there and wash, but they warned us not to drink the water. The Japs didn't drink the water either because they were afraid of it, afraid it was contaminated. I think one of the reasons was that most of their gardens were fertilized by human waste. They had straddle-trenches even in Japan-concrete ones, and ever so often one of those things would get full and they'd send what we called a honey-cart around and they'd unload. They had a big bucket with a long handle on it and they'd scoop this human waste out of the straddle trenches and dump them on this honey cart which they used to fertilize their gardens and their yard and everything. I'm sure that's why they wouldn't drink the water, but I'd get so dog-gone thirsty for a drink of cold water, I'd go in there at night and get me a drink of cold water. It might have helped me, it might have had some vitamins in it for all I know, I never did get sick from drinking it, and no one else knew that I drank it," said Ruse.

"We'd get off of work, and the Japs that worked in the plant over there with us lived in a little village close to the plant and there was a road that ran right by the front of our prison camp. Of course we had a solid, black wall up there that was about ten or twelve feet tall and we were inside that wall. Beside the road there after you got out of the factory, there was a big building. It was a large, cement tub; it was as large as the building was. The whole inside of the building was, I'd say, about thirty to forty feet square and about four feet deep. They'd all jump in there, men, women, and kids would all jump in there and take a bath before they went home. Of course, we didn't get a chance to do anything like that," said Ruse.

"We had one fellow in there in our camp in Japan, he was about half crazy. Something was wrong with him. He'd get so hungry that he couldn't help himself, I guess. The Jap guards there at the guardhouse always brought their lunch in a little metal pale, and every day this boy would steal one of their lunches," said Ruse.

"When they finally caught him once doing that, any time one was missing, they'd go get him and they'd take two of these big wooden rice buckets which weighed about five to ten pounds each and fill them full of sand, and had a rice, straw rope between the buckets and hang them over his shoulders and make him run around the compound until he dropped. He was probably carrying fifty pounds at least on his shoulders. In the shape he was in, he couldn't go very far, and they were running along behind him poking him with bayonets and sticks and things. They did that nearly every day until we finally got out of there," said Ruse.

"We had one boy in there named Whittle. He was one of about two or three hundred Englishmen who had been in Singapore. Whittle was an English Sergeant and he would have some kind of a fit where he would have superhuman strengths," said Ruse. "He'd just get up and start running. I saw him run through a wooden door one time, just splintered the thing. He never knew what happened, when he'd come out of it, wouldn't remember anything that happened. It would affect him in different ways. Sometimes he couldn't open his eyes, sometimes he couldn't talk. One time I know one of the little guards came up to him and made motions to let him know that he knew he was the one that had those fits and Whittle said, "Yeah, you slant-eyed so and so, I'd like to have you in front of me when I have one of my fits."

"Rice was all we got there in Japan to eat, and when they got low on rice they started feeding us barley, which is even worse than rice. Rice is more or less edible, but that barley, it's like eating a handful of straw. We would get up and go to work every morning, and come in at noon for about thirty minutes to eat a half a bowl of rice. They gave us what amounted to about the size of one of our chili bowls, regular chili bowls that you get in a café," said Ruse. That was packed with cooked rice for two men, and there was some of the darndest measuring you ever saw in your life when they divided that bowl of rice up between the two. They'd get down and measure, and sometimes I even thought they counted the grains." Frank Sametheni, a Dutch POW at Yokkaichi, remembered the method used to split a double ration of barley as follows: "There is no discrimination whatsoever; everyone gets what is due to him. Even the knife used to split the cooked ball of barley in two halves may not be licked clean by the same person. His helper is to lick the other side."[c]

V

Over twelve hundred nautical miles away, on the white coral island of Tinian the men of the 509th waited for the mission that they had been trained for, and yet most of them knew very few specific details about. Only a select few of them were aware of their ultimate purpose. Then, on July 16th, at the White Sands Proving Ground in the New Mexican desert, the "Trinity" detonation demonstrated that the Manhattan Project had done what it had aimed to do. The atomic age had arrived.[7]

In Japan, air raids and incendiary bombings were happening daily. Cities were being burned to the ground, being reduced to ash, yet this was nowhere near the destruction that was to come.

---

[c] From the online autobiography of Frank Samethini. "The Sky Looked Down: A Memoir of the Burma Railway" Retrieved from URL: http://theskylookeddown.blogspot.com/ on 4-3-2010

Photo of Yokkaichi Prison Camp taken soon after the end of the war. Carl Ruse is visible in the photo standing on the beach, waving at the planes. He is standing with two other POWs, and is seen waving his crutches made from two-by-fours. Ruse obtained the photo years after his liberation after meeting a friend who knew someone who was on the plane that took the photos.

CHAPTER XI

A SIXTY-DEGREE BANK

They who sow the wind shall reap the typhoon.

Philippine proverb

With a new and unprecedented weapon at his disposal, President Truman, now knew that he held a power that was never before known to man, with which he could quickly end the war. The day after the Trinity detonation, Truman was attending the Potsdam Conference along with Joseph Stalin and Winston Churchill. The three were gathered to make decisions on how to handle Nazi-Germany after the death of Hitler and establish a post-war order. By previous agreement made by Stalin and Roosevelt at the Yalta Conference in February, communist Russia was to enter the war with Japan within ninety days of the end of the war in Europe, however, Truman now knew that the war could be won without the help of Stalin. With his new power, and no longer needing Stalin as an ally, Truman approached the conference with a renewed sense of authority. He wanted to end the war before being forced to use Stalin, whom he had become disenchanted with, as an ally.

In his memoirs, President Truman wrote on July 24th, "I casually mentioned to Stalin that we had a new weapon of unusual destructive force. The Russian premier showed no special interest. All he said was that he was glad to hear it and hoped we would make "…good use of it against the Japanese."[1] Japan's defeat was clear already, however, it was the *surrender* of Japan that Truman needed. Without surrender, the deaths of Americans would continue. If an American invasion of the Japanese homeland were to come to be, the cost in American lives was estimated to be astronomical. Since March, fifty thousand American lives had been lost. From his perspective, Truman might have wondered how he could justify *not* using the weapon to the American people and exponentially increasing that awful number, especially after all of the dollars that had been spent on the Manhattan Project.[2]

By July 25th, an American cruiser, the *Indianapolis* was in Tinian Harbor, unloading components of the atomic bomb. The same day, the Allies issued the Potsdam Declaration, a final warning and ultimatum to the Japanese empire.[3]

The thirteen points of the declaration outlined the terms of unconditional Japanese surrender and ended with the line: "*The alternative for Japan is prompt and utter destruction.*" There were no surprises in the Potsdam Declaration for the Japanese leaders. Many of their cities were already being burned, and the atomic bomb was a new and unknown threat.

In response to the declaration, the Japanese employed the word "*mokusatsu*" which, translated to English, means "take no notice of; treat (anything) with silent contempt; ignore [by keeping silence]; remain in a wise and masterly inactivity."[a] When reporters in Tokyo questioned Japanese Premier Kantaro Suzuki about his government's reaction to the Potsdam Declaration, he replied that he was *withholding comment*, using the word, *mokusatsu*. While it is plausible that Suzuki's intent was simply to keep quiet since no formal decision pertaining to the declaration had been made by

---

[a] -Kenkyusha's *New* Japanese - English Dictionary, p.1129.

Japanese leadership, after the word was translated internationally, the world heard that the declaration was "not worthy of comment." Two days later, Suzuki reinforced the meaning of the word as it had been interpreted internationally by repeating it at a press conference. The ambiguity of his word choice, interpreted as arrogance incensed international leaders who felt that the Japanese were no longer in a place to bargain.

By July 31st, the bomb components were stored in heavily-guarded huts on the island of Tinian. A cable was sent to Washington: "Lemay needs eleven hours more which would be August 1, 1000 hours of E.W.T." After that, the bomb would be ready for drop over Japan.[4]

It was the 9th of July, 1945 when Ruse heard an air-raid siren in the prison camp at Yokkaichi and saw B-29's overhead: "Finally the air raids really got started good and the Japs had a bomb shelter for the guards. When it was just a general raid, these long blasts on the sirens would keep on going, but when they saw the planes were coming in our direction and it was going to be a local raid, these short blasts would start," said Ruse. "When that happened, the guards had a bomb shelter and all went underground. Well, when they did that, we could step out and watch the fireworks."

"One night we saw a P-51 dive down a searchlight beam and shoot the light out; then the boys could start coming over in those B-29s with their landing lights on. That shows how scared they were. The Jap planes, they would only buzz around during the day when there was no air raid going on, but when there was an air raid and the siren went off, boy, they made themselves scarce. They went over to the backside of the island, I guess. I once asked one of those guards that could speak a little English, what happened to their planes when there was an air raid. He said they were saving them for the invasion. At that time, they were expecting the Americans to invade Japan," said Ruse.

"One night, the night the B-29s that were doing the bombing that burned Yokkaichi down,[b] the planes came right over

---

[b] Yokkaichi was incendiary-bombed on July 9, 1945. 567 B-29s participated in this bombing.

Retrieved from URL: http://atomicbombmuseum.org/2_manhattan.shtml on 2-16-2010 our camp about seven O'clock, just about dark, just about sunset, and until daylight the next morning there was a flight of B-29s overhead all night long. There was never a lull in it," said Ruse.

"They would drop these napalm bombs just about right over our camp and they would fall forward about three hundred yards across the water from us and hit Yokkaichi, and when they hit they spread out over a wide area and they burned everything in their path," said Ruse. "They looked like flares or burning Christmas trees as they fell to the ground. That was really something. I wouldn't take anything for having seen that. We were about half way between the two cities of Nagoya[c] and Osaka and we stood out and watched them burn. It was quite a show to see a bunch of B-29s dropping fire-bombs on those cities. I just hope that something like that never happens here."

"They were releasing the bombs right over us, but I don't think a man in there was worried about it because I don't know, you get in a situation like that, you just don't care. In fact a lot of times, you wish one of them did fall in on you," said Ruse. "Finally, *finally*, they quit about daylight the next morning and we weren't bothered too much by air-raids anymore. They came around pretty close, but they didn't bomb right in our immediate vicinity."

II

On August 4th, the men of the 509th on Tinian filed into a briefing room. Seven crews watched a film of a giant mushroom cloud rise up into the New Mexico sky, turning darkness into a blinding light. The reason for their peculiar training and secrecy was finally clear. The film had been shot only nineteen days earlier. Colonel Paul Tibbets then briefed the men on procedures for the first flight, including schedules, and routes for the mission.[5]

---

[c] Nagoya was the location of Mitsubishi Aircraft Engine Works, and was industrial center for steel, automobile, and wartime weapons industries.

A Sixty-Degree Bank

The next day, Sunday, August 5th, the dangerous job of assembling the bomb began. Two pieces of the deadly Uranium-235 were positioned at opposite ends of the casing. An explosive charge was placed behind one of them that would blast the piece toward the other with the velocity of a bullet.

On the sixth of August, Colonel Tibbets departed to Japan with the assembled bomb, codenamed "Little Boy" in the bomb bay of the *Enola Gay*. At 7:30 A.M., they spotted the Japanese coastline; headed for Hiroshima. At a point sixty miles from the target, Tibbets turned west, and by 8:15 A.M., the plane would be directly over the city.

At 8:14 A.M., the bomb was released from the hefty plane and Tibbets immediately pulled into a steep sixty degree bank to avoid the intensity of the explosion. When the bomb had fallen to an altitude of 1,890 feet the cordite explosive sent the cylindrical U-235 casing barreling to the other end of the bomb, colliding with the other cylinder. When the two collided, the resulting explosion caused a blinding light and the temperature over Hiroshima jumped to be that of the sun. The shock wave from the blast rippled out from the epicenter, leveling structures on the ground. The city had not been previously incendiary-bombed as other cities had; it was left as a pristine target. Tens of thousands of people were instantly dead or about to die.

After the plane leveled, the men on the *Enola Gay* could see the devastation below. Lighting his pipe, Tibbets pointed the plane back towards Tinian, and said "I think this is the end of the War."[6]

Yokkaichi Prison Camp as seen on August 28th, 1945. Note prisoners standing outside of prison gates. Courtesy Bill Briggs; *HMS Indefatigable.*

III

President Truman heard the news while traveling home from Potsdam on board the cruiser *Augusta*. An aide handed a note to the President:

"Big bomb dropped on Hiroshima August 5 at 7:15 P.M. Washington time. First reports indicate complete success which was even more conspicuous than earlier test."

On the afternoon of August 7th, the *Augusta* made port at Norfolk, and then Truman took a special train to Washington. By the 8th of August, the world knew that Truman had returned to D.C. There was still no word from Japan, nor any immediate sign of surrender.[7]

As initial reports of the destruction in Hiroshima made there way to Japan, military leadership was frantic to learn more about the bomb. The same day, an American flyer, Lieutenant Marcus McDilda was shot down over Japan on a strafing mission and captured. He was marched blindfolded through city streets and civilians beat him as he passed. That night he was brought to a Police Headquarters in Osaka for interrogation. He was asked about his home base at Iwo Jima. He responded by lying about details of the P-51 which he flew, as well as details about the number of planes located on Iwo Jima. When his interrogators produced photographs that trapped him in his lie about the number of planes on Iwo Jima, the flyer received another beating.

As questioning became more intense, interrogators began asking McDilda what he knew of the atomic bomb. McDilda knew absolutely nothing of the weapon. At one point, a general entered the room and jabbed a sword forward through McDilda's lip. He screamed: "If you don't tell me about the bomb, I'll personally cut off your head." The pilot wondered what he could tell them to save his own life. He began:

"As you know, when atoms are split, there are a lot of plusses and minuses are released. Well, we've taken these and put them in a huge container and separated them from each other with a lead shield. When the box is dropped out of the plane, we melt the lead shield and the pluses and minuses come together. When that happens it causes a tremendous bolt of lightning and all of the atmosphere over a city is pushed back! Then when the atmosphere rolls back, it brings about a tremendous thunderclap, which knocks down everything beneath it!" McDilda ended by telling the interrogators that Tokyo would be bombed during the next few days, and continued the ridiculous story to the amazed and appalled officers. The tale made its way to Japanese Military leadership, who informed the cabinet of the grim news, and still ultimately refused immediate surrender until after a second bomb was dropped on Nagasaki.[8]

In discussions with Admiral William Purnell, General Groves expressed that he felt that dropping one bomb was not enough; it would take two bombs to abruptly end the war. They wanted the Japanese to know that the weapon was in production.

Apparently, President Truman agreed. Plans for the second atomic mission were quickly made. Major Chuck Sweeney was to fly another B-29, *Bocks Car* for the drop. Weather was poor that night, but the decision was made to move forward with the mission anyway. Kokura was the primary target, and Nagasaki had been designated as an alternate. After passing over a target that was obstructed by haze, and seeing anti-aircraft flak, as well as fighters attempting to climb to intercept the bomber, Sweeney made the call to move on to Nagasaki. Critically low on fuel, Sweeney had to take a direct route to Nagasaki, further risking detection.

In Nagasaki on August 9th, two hundred thousand people worked as usual. The Mitsubishi war plants manufactured torpedoes and small arms for the Japanese war efforts. They worked at full-capacity; well aware that an invasion was likely in the future.

With only enough fuel for one pass over Nagasaki, the B-29 dropped its payload over Nagasaki, exploding at an altitude just over 1,500 feet. Immediately after dropping the payload, the crews made a steep and abrupt turn, headed away from the blast towards Okinawa; they had too little fuel to return to Tinian. Headed towards Okinawa unexpectedly, Sweeney attempted to contact the tower on the ground but got no response. The crew had been at the controls for over twelve hours, and with so little fuel, there was no time to circle. Sweeney guided the plane into a direct descent.

As they approached, they saw squadrons of B-25s and P-38s taking off and landing below. At Sweeney's order, the crew began unloading the plane's flares, attempting to gain the attention of the ground crew. Finally, the flares attracted enough attention to clear the way below, and the B-29 touched down hard, narrowly missing a row of planes parked to the side.

The crew spent less than two hours on Okinawa. After refueling, they headed back to Tinian; arriving nearly twenty hours after their mission began.[9]

IV

In Washington, Truman was due to give a radio address to the American people on Potsdam:

"I realize the tragic significance of the atomic bomb. It's production and it's use were not lightly undertaken by this government. But we knew that our enemies were on a search for it... We won the race of discovery against the Germans. Having found the bomb we have used it. We have used it against those who attacked us without warning at Pearl Harbor, against those who have starved and beaten and executed American prisoners of war, against those who have abandoned all pretense of obeying international laws of warfare. We have used it to shorten the agony of war, in order to save the lives of thousands and thousands of young Americans. We shall continue to use it until we completely destroy Japan's power to make war. Only a Japanese surrender will stop us."[10]

Only hours after the bombing, in an air-raid shelter in Tokyo, Japan's inner cabinet representing various branches of government and military had assembled to meet with the Emperor. The tense assembly had come together to discuss the dreaded possibility of surrender. There was bitter debate about how the war would end, some wishing to fight on through a final invasion. However, concern came up about the testimony from McDilda, the fighter pilot who had been captured days before that Tokyo could be the next target for an atomic bomb. The possibility that he could have been telling the truth was a frightening reality. Japanese resources were all but depleted, and attempts at defense would likely end with total loss. Finally, Emperor Hirohito rose and spoke, aiming to break the impasse among the cabinet:

"I agree with the Foreign Minister's plan. I have given serious thought to the situation prevailing at home and abroad and have concluded that continuing the war can only mean destruction for the nation and a prolongation of bloodshed and cruelty in the world. Those who argue for continuing the war once assured me that new battalions and supplies would be ready at Kujikurihama by June. I realize now that this cannot be fulfilled even by September. As for those who wish for one last battle here on our own soil, let me remind them of the disparity between their previous plans and what has actually taken place. I cannot bear to see my innocent people struggle any longer. Ending the war is the only way to restore world peace and to relieve the nation from the terrible distress with which it is burdened..." The Emperor ended his speech by saying: "When I think of the feelings of my Imperial Grandfather, Emperor Meiji, at the time of the Triple Intervention, I cannot but swallow my tears and sanction the proposal to accept the Allied Proclamation on the basis outlined by the Foreign Minister."[11]

Hirohito went to the door that had been opened by his aide, and was gone. The role of Emperor had traditionally been a ceremonial one; he technically did not have a vote in the final decision, but the weight of his influence was significant. By 4:00 A.M., a final decision was made by the cabinet; Japan would surrender. The only stipulation of the surrender would be that the Emperor keep his ceremonial status. Within hours, the Foreign Ministry began sending the news in code for transmittal to officials in the Allied capitals.[12]

Val Bennett's photograph of POW Camp at Yokkaichi – August 1945

Yokkaichi Prison Camp with POW's standing on beach. Scrawled in the sand with what is presumed to be stones was the inscription: " YANKS 196 BR 25 DU" – taken to be American, British and Dutch POWs. Courtesy of Bill Briggs; *HMS Indefatigable.*

We Volunteered

CHAPTER XII

HELL TO HEAVEN

The whole earth is at rest, and is
quiet: they break forth into singing.
ISAIAH 14:7

P resident Truman called military officials for a meeting
at the White House at 9:00 A.M., Washington time
on August 10th. Before 10:00 A.M., Secretary of State
James F. Byrnes and Henry Stimson, Secretary of War, began
discussing the wording of a reply to the Japanese surrender
transmission. During this conversation Stimson noted an urgent
request from General George Marshall; *Allied prisoners should be
released immediately and moved to an accessible area of Japan.*

In July, General Marshall had sent a message to Washington
from China expressing concerns about prisoners behind Japanese
lines. Meanwhile, outside on Pennsylvania Avenue and in Lafayette
Park, large crowds were beginning to gather as rumors of the end of
war spread from person to person. The people were waiting to
rejoice with the first declaration of end to the war that had lasted so
long.

By the end of the day the final draft of this statement was being readied for transmission to Tokyo.[1]

II

It was August 11th in Fukuoka, only one hundred miles of the devastated city of Nagasaki where the Japanese held eight captives who were the crew of a B-29 that had been downed recently. At 8:30 A.M. in the morning the men were loaded into a truck and driven down the road. They stopped several miles south of the city at a place called Aburayama and were taken from the truck and lined up where they watched their captors begin digging large holes in the ground.

One of the men was taken out of the line, and forced to his knees. As his comrades watched, a Japanese soldier drew his sword and raised it over his head, bringing it down on the neck of the crewman, very nearly severing his head. One by one, the men in the line watched as their friends were killed; all the time knowing that their turn was coming. With each murder, their captor used different and more painful methods of execution.

The final man, after watching seven other men die, was forced to the ground, just as the others were. From ten feet away, a Japanese man raised a bow and arrow, pulled back, took aim and sent an arrow flying towards the man's head. The first two arrows missed their target, whizzing past his face. The third arrow landed just above his left eye. Still alive, he was brought to his knees, where his captors chopped his head from his body.[2]

In Tokyo, military leadership was split on how to react to the American response. Many of the men wanted to continue to fight, and discussions of revolt were taking place. Some wanted to fight to the death of each and every citizen in the country. Meanwhile, in areas surrounding Nagasaki, people were dying even more frequently as their bodies were being destroyed internally from the radiation which they had been exposed to.

Early in the morning on August 15th, Japanese War Minister Korechika Anami knew that the Japanese must surrender and that a coup against the Emperor in attempt to continue to fight would ultimately fail. Anami committed suicide by *seppuku*[a] and died a slow and painful death.

III

In Washington, President Truman stood at his desk in the oval office in front of a room full of photographers, military officials, and statesmen. Truman read from a paper in his hand:

> "I have just received a note from the Japanese Government in reply to the message forwarded to that Government by the Secretary of State on August 11th. I deem this reply a full acceptance of the Potsdam Declaration which specifies the unconditional surrender of Japan."

Outside the White House crowds rejoiced as the President appeared and addressed the people that lined the fence there. The crowd cheered every sentence of the brief speech, and then Truman stepped back inside to phone his mother. The nationwide celebration spread into the night. Across the United States, the party was on. Contrastingly in Japan of course, the POW's there had still been going to work as slaves in factories and continued to starve in captivity and fight for their lives.

That day in Japan, the people heard the Emperor speak to them over the radio, an unprecedented occurrence that opposed national tradition. The civilians crowded around radios with heads down as they listened to the Emperor say that the fighting would be over. They would surrender.

In Fukuoka, where eight B-29 crewmen had been murdered only four days earlier, sixteen more airmen were driven in a truck away from their POW camp and died the same bloody death as the

---

[a] *Seppuku* is suicide by cutting the stomach (Hari Kiri).

other crew. The executions were kept secret because the crew members knew too much. Their captors were concerned that if a trial for war-crimes were to occur, they would say that they had seen other healthy POWs disappear and not return only days before the war was over. The sixteen men died whilst meanwhile in the United States, the nation was breaking out in celebration because the war was over.

In Yokkaichi, Ruse, who was still in the prison camp hospital due to his broken foot, noticed the sudden cessation of the daily air raids. "We thought that was kind of odd and we were hoping that something had happened. The boys all had gone to work after noon and then came right back in and we knew something was up. The air-raids had stopped, and we figured that the war was over, that they had surrendered. We didn't know until the next day what really happened, but the Japs came around and gave us some sugar and some Jap cigarettes. So we knew something big was up, and the next day after they gave us those, we found out that the war was really over, that the Japs had surrendered."

The news came the next day when Avengers off of an aircraft carrier flew over and made an air drop. Preparations for the supply drop had been underway onboard the *HMS Indefatigable* for days already as a brief typhoon postponed a supply drop. Onboard *Indefatigable*, large bags were sewn and attached to the Royal Air Force observer-type parachutes. The ship had been at sea since departing from Sydney on the 7th of July, and luxuries onboard were sparse.[b] "The planes dropped some supplies to us, and you could tell these boys just cleaned out their footlockers and sent it to us," said Ruse. "They came over and dropped a little parachute with a piece of plywood on it with a note on it, and they were off that British Aircraft Carrier, *Indefatigable*. The war had come to an end so suddenly that they were about out of supplies themselves. They were past time for them to go to Australia to replenish their supplies. They sent some canned food and a half tube of toothpaste or something like that, and that really showed they cleaned out their lockers for us."

---

[b] Roy Hawkes, HMS Indefatigable

Avengers from the *HMS Indefatigable make the very first supply drops to POWs at Yokkaichi.* Note the falling parachutes, and POWs on the beach. Courtesy Roy Hawkes.

The following day, B-29s flew over Yokkaichi and dropped food and clothing in fifty five gallon drums with parachutes to the men on the ground. "They dropped enough supplies on us that we could've lived two years on, I'm sure," said Ruse.

"The first thing I ate, I took a G.I. tin helmet and put a little can of sliced peaches in it and a tall can of condensed milk and stirred it all up and ate the whole thing," said Ruse. "I figured it would make me sick, but it never did, but that was the first thing I ate. After we got those, some of the boys went around gathering up all of the Jap sugar and cigarettes they gave us, and took them over and piled them in front of the Jap guardhouse and burned them in front of them. And the Japs didn't have much of that stuff themselves. But the Japs, especially the ones that we would like to have seen after the war, had already disappeared. They made themselves scarce, especially the interpreter because he was a sorry fellow. He always did his best to make us feel worse."

POW's at the railway station at Arai, Japan, awaiting transportation to the *USS Rescue.* Courtesy of Wes Injerd

The Prisoners remained at Yokkaichi for a full week after the surrender until they were finally able to leave by train. "They made the Japs put all of this surplus food and supplies that the B-29s dropped on that same train so we could take them back and we didn't leave anything for them," said Ruse. "But that little boy that used to slip food to me, I left a lot of food with him. And there were a lot of Koreans who worked there with us and we gave them a lot of it," said Ruse. Ruse said goodbye to the young boy for the last time without ever knowing his name.

"General MacArthur had given orders to the Japs to put in a radio in each one of the camps because he wanted to speak to all of the POWs the next day at noon," said Ruse. He told us that the war was over but we were to stay right where we were. He said if you get out among these Jap Civilians, they're not very happy about the outcome of the war and you might get into a lot of trouble. That night, I was over in this makeshift hospital we had and there was a Sailor that slept next to me and he slipped out that night and went over to a Jap village over next to where we were, and he came home about two o'clock in the morning, and was in a lot of pain. He died at about four o'clock, and we just figured that the Japs had probably given him some saké that was poisoned."

"Finally they gave the Japs orders to load us up on the train and take us over to a place on the coast called Hamamatsu. When we got to Hamamatsu, there were these snub-nosed Navy landing crafts there waiting for us, and we loaded up on those and it took us out to a Navy Hospital Ship," said Ruse.

"The *USS Rescue*[c] was the name of the ship we were picked up on. We walked up the ladder at the top of the ship, and at the top there was two big husky fellows," said Ruse. "They made us strip down and throw everything we had into the ocean. I was on the crutches that Cecil Crouch, had made for me. They threw them in the ocean and gave me a pair of real crutches. They took us in and made us get in a shower. They de-loused us and gave us some clean clothes, and we went in and they put us all in bunks. The first thing I ate there was a steak. I was surprised. They asked what we wanted to eat, and that's what I told them I wanted. I didn't figure that I'd get it, but I did, and I really did enjoy it."

---

[c] The *USS Rescue* was a converted passenger liner previously named *Antaeus*. Upon the conclusion of World War II, *Rescue* sailed into Tokyo Bay with the 3rd Fleet and began the medical screening of Allied prisoners of war and shuttling them from various prison camps to the base at Yokohama. In late September, the ship arrived at Guam where she discharged a few former prisoners whose home had been on that island. *Rescue* then proceeded to San Francisco, CA. She was decommissioned on 29 June 1946 and was transferred to the Maritime Administration. Her name was struck from the Navy list on 15 August 1946. The vessel was subsequently refitted as a merchant ship and saw service as such from 1946 into 1959, in which year she was scrapped.

Retrieved from URL: http://www.history.navy.mil/danfs/a9/antaeus.htm on 2-17-2010

We Volunteered

After getting fed and cleaned up and immediate needs addressed aboard the ship, the men caught up on three and a half years of news at home and were eager to get in contact with their families, most of who had no idea if they were alive or dead, or simply assumed that they were in fact dead.

The first letter Carl Ruse wrote as a liberated man was to his father:

Dear Dad:
I don't know how to start this since it is the first letter I have written in 3 and a half years.
I hope everyone is well. I am fine. I will be able to walk again by the time we reach the states.
We boarded the ship day before yesterday. It was like going from Hell to Heaven. I ate two fried eggs for supper, my first eggs in three years. I am still afraid that this is all a dream, that I will suddenly awaken and find some slant-eyed bastard yelling at me.
I can't tell you when we are starting home or where I will be when I do arrive in the states but I will wire my address as soon as possible. We are lying about three miles off shore near a small place called Hamamatsu on the eastern coast near the center of the island of Honshu.
Everyone is nice to us. They won't let us do a thing for ourselves. This is really swell after having been shut off from the civilized world for so long.
Hope you can read this. I am lying on my bunk - a bunk with sheets, a mattress, and pillows!
We saw a movie last night. It was a "horse opera", but we enjoyed it.
I think I will be allowed to come home shortly after arriving in the States. I hope we won't be treated like a bunch of outcasts. We are being checked for diseases of all kinds. Malaria has given me more trouble than anything. I believe that is cured now though. I have taken as many grains of quinine as I have eaten grains of rice, and I have eaten rice three meals a day while a P.O.W.
I hope to be with you Thanksgiving Day if not sooner. I am really looking forward to it. I will probably be a bit misty-eyed, but it can't be helped. I saw my first American flag the other day and I've got to say that my eyes were a bit moist.
I am sending this to the address you gave in your letter. Please notify everyone that I will see them soon.
        Love, Carl
P.S. Planes from the H.M.S. "Indefatigable" found our camp and dropped food to us. It is the only British aircraft carrier in these waters. Please do me a big favor and wire my thanks along with that of 296 other P.O.W. from the Japanese P.O.W. Camp at Yokkaichi to the Commander of the "Indefatigable". Those boys voluntarily cut their own rations in order to give us food and cigarettes. We quit eating rice and seaweed and started eating real food.

158

Please try to find out if my Squadron Commander Capt. (Maj.?) W.E. Dyess from Albany Texas reached the States. He escaped and I heard rumors that he arrived in the States. I hope so. He would have gone a long way in the war if he had had a chance. Will wire as soon as I reach the States.

Ruse had to learn the difficult news that his greatly admired leader, Ed Dyess had died after making it back to the states.

Ruse had been away from the world for so long, he had missed much of the goings-on in the domestic world. Ruse wrote to Dyess' mother of her son, and she kindly responded by sending him the newspaper articles about her son's return from captivity, and his accidental death. After enduring all that he had, and then escaping at Davao, Dyess was killed in a plane crash in California after developing engine trouble. Rather than potentially harm civilians on the ground attempting to land, he turned the plane and saved the lives of others. He had been buried in his hometown of Albany, Texas.

While spending several days on the hospital ship, plans were being made to begin the long journey back to the States, and then Ruse was taken to Yokohama where he disembarked for processing. "We were supposed to get on an Army hospital ship to come back to the states, when I noticed a long line of fellows lined up outside at a building there," said Ruse. "I didn't know what it was all about, so I asked them what they were lined up for and they said that there was a medical office in there that examined everyone. Those that were able to fly, they were going to let them fly back to the Philippines. I fell in line, too."

As Ruse came towards the front of the line, he saw that there was a Captain there interviewing men when they came through. "The ones that were able to fly, or that he considered to be able to fly, he let 'em fly back to Okinawa. When he got to me he said, 'You think you're able to fly?' I said 'Yes Sir I can!' He said, 'You might have to walk a long ways.', but I had already seen there was a G.I. truck outside loading the guys on the truck so I knew I wasn't going to have to walk very far," said Ruse. "They took us out to the airstrip and we boarded a plane about midnight that night and flew over to Okinawa. I will never forget that night."

"It was the best... the prettiest flight I was *ever* in. We were way up above some thunderheads in an electrical storm and the lightning was flashing down below us in the clouds and it was quite a sight," said Ruse. "Finally, when we landed at Okinawa at about 3:00 or 3:30, Loya and I were singled out, and a couple of Hospital Corpsmen came over and got him and came and got me and loaded us on an ambulance. I told them I could walk alright, but they said that it was alright and that they were told to pick us up, and there was two ambulances and a bunch of GI trucks."

"Loya and I were singled out, and instead of going to the tents where the other guys were taken, we went to the Red Cross tent, and there was some Red Cross girls lined up on both sides of that place giving you anything you wanted-razors, razor blades; anything," said Ruse. "There were some nurses over there. They had cokes and donuts. Boy, those were the best cokes and donuts I ever ate. We stayed there till daylight then they took us over to where the rest were."

"We were in tents and it had been raining, and boy, in Okinawa, it rains a lot. Those crutches would sink down in that mud and I had a heck of a time getting around. So we'd go over to the mess hall (they had a big old tent for mess hall). They'd come out and get me and Loya and take us in and take a tray to go through the line and get our food for us," said Ruse.

Photo # 80-G-439636   USS Rescue underway on 2 March 1945

USS Rescue underway on march 2nd, 1945. National Archives.

"I soon discovered they had a bunch of Jap prisoners working around that mess hall," said Ruse. "So I went out there where they were and the first time I talked to one of them I said, *"Your house-o, where?"* He finally let me know what town he lived in in Japan, and I said, "Too bad, too bad, American Skokie fly over and Nagoya no more." Whatever town he told me. I had a lot of fun doing that."

"After three days there in Okinawa, they gave us some new clothes, then loaded us into a plane going to Manila. When we started to take off, we got up off the ground about ten feet, I guess, that plane kind of went down and bounced around and bounced around, and he finally got it stopped," said Ruse. "That little old pilot came walking down the aisle from the cockpit. He was white as a sheet. I wondered what in the world was wrong with him. One of the motors on that plane (it was a two-motored plane, a C-46, I think it was), conked out and they couldn't get up any higher. He finally got it, got it on the ground and got it stopped. I wondered why he was so was so scared. When we got off the plane, we were about twenty feet from the end of the runway and it just dropped straight down to the China Sea, about two-hundred yards. I could see why he was so white when he walked out there, but they worked on that plane awhile and we got back on and took off again and we flew on over to the Philippines."

"I was in two different hospitals there in Manila for about a month, and one day old Loya came in to see me and said, 'I'm getting ready to go home.' I said, 'You are?' He said, 'I'll send you a Christmas card.' I said 'Okay.' They were going by ship. The next couple of days the doctor asked me if I felt like flying and I told him yes. He said I'm going to let you fly on back home. I don't remember how many days it was, but it two or three days before we planned to come home. On the way back, we landed a Guam first and spent the night there."

"We also landed in Kwajalein, which is a little tiny island out in the middle of the Pacific. Flying in, it didn't look like the tallest place on the island was five feet at the highest point. I always wondered what they did in case they ever got into a typhoon like we got into while going to Japan," said Ruse. "There was a boy out of the Air Transport Command sitting next to me in this C-54. He said; 'We're going to land at Kwajalein in about ten minutes.' I said, 'Kwajalein, what's that?'

He said, "It's an island out there." I said, "I don't see any place to land." "Right down there," said Ruse. "I looked and it looked like a matchstick floating on water." I said, "We're going to land on that?" He said "Yeah, You come in off the water and hit the runway just after you get past the water and you get stopped right at the other end of the runway, just before you go into the water again."

Ambulances lined up at the 120th General Hospital, Manila, waiting to pick up and evacuate American patients to the United States. Print from Air Evaluation Board, Orlando Army Air Base.

"We stopped there and gassed up," said Ruse. "Then we went onto Honolulu. We took off about midnight from Honolulu for San Francisco and that sure was a pretty town to fly over," said Ruse. "It sure was a pretty place."

"While over the ocean between Honolulu and San Francisco, all of a sudden the plane just dropped. The boy next to me, was in the Air Transport Command (Air Transport was an outfit that flew supplies over that hump in India, those Himalayas, from India into China during the war)," said Ruse.

"When that plane dropped he said, 'How far do you think we dropped?' 'I don't know, about ten or fifteen feet,' said Ruse. 'More like a close to half a mile,' the man replied. Then he started telling me how they would get those aircraft over there in the Himalayas. The plane would drop, he said, sometimes several miles before it ever stopped, and a lot of times, they wondered if it was ever going to stop, but of course, they were up maybe forty thousand feet."

"When we flew into San Francisco from Honolulu coming home, on a hill out there, on Angel Island, they had a sign that said 'Welcome Home. Well Done.' There was big, white rocks that formed those letters and they were painted with white paint, and the boy out of the air transport command sitting next to me in the plane said 'They've got that right.' He said 'Anyone who's been where we've been, it was well done.'"[d]

"We landed then at Hamilton Air Base there where I started out from. I don't know whether all these guys on that plane were crippled or not, but I think we all were. They took us by ambulance on into the Letterman Hospital[e] at San Francisco."[f]

---

[d] Angel Island was an embarkation site for troops headed toward the Pacific war zone during World War II and a processing facility for prisoners of war. When troops returned from the war, a 60-foot sign with the illuminated words "Welcome Home, Well Done" greeted them from the island.

Retrieved from URL: http://angelisland.org/wp-content/uploads/2010/01/Brochure-Angel-Island-State-Park.pdf

[e] During World War II, Letterman's location made it the most important hospital for the treatment of sick and wounded soldiers from the Pacific Theater. The statistics are staggering—in 1945 alone Letterman General Hospital received more than 73,000 patients. Towards the end of the war, a small stockade for Italian and German prisoners

Hell to Heaven

"At Letterman hospital there in San Francisco, they had big, open ice boxes full of cracked ice and full of cartons of milk, and we could go out and help ourselves and drink all the milk we wanted," said Ruse. "I bet I drank six or eight quarts every day. One day after I'd been in there, I guess maybe a week a bunch of guys came walking in there and old Loya was in the middle of them. I thought he was going to pass out when he saw me laying there in the bed! I asked him, 'Are you still going to send me that Christmas card?'

V

After recovering at Letterman, Ruse was finally released to return home to Texas. It had been four years since he had even so much as visited the place or seen his family. In the same way that a train had taken him into a new era of his life fifteen years earlier, he was headed home at last; and once again, a train ride would pick him up in one stage of his life only to drop him off in the next. It had been years since the open freight car had deposited him in California. How fitting that his homecoming would carry him along many miles of the same tracks.

The train would be headed to a Hospital in Temple, Texas, which was closer to family. The accommodations on the train were more than sufficient to please a man who had on his previous train rides been crammed into a boxcar as freight that had less value than that of a head of livestock. "I'd never seen a railroad car like that before. They had big long windows and our bunks were right level

---

was established at Letterman; these POW's provided labor for the hospital during their brief internment.

Retrieved from URL: http://www.nps.gov/prsf/historyculture/letterman-complex-page-2.htm

[f] The first POWs arrived at San Francisco on September 2nd 1945. By the end of the year the hospital had processed 3,780 of these POWs.

Retrieved from URL: http://www.militarymuseum.org/LettermanAMC.html

with the windows. We'd just lay there and watch the scenery as we went by. I sure enjoyed that trip," said Ruse.

Chapter XIII

Vagabond House

When we assumed the soldier we did not lay aside the citizen.

General George Washington
June 26, 1775

Carl Ruse returned from the Second World War after months of brutal fighting and having been a captive for over forty one months. His captors had dished out endless torture, beatings, violence, and forced labor, yet, despite everything they could do to him, he had been its equal. He had equaled everything they could throw at him, and more. Looking into the eyes of the prison photo taken by captors upon his arrival in Japan, it is easy to imagine what he might have been thinking. The eyes are stern and hard. They are direct; looking straight into the lens with a burning focus, daring onlookers to look him in the eye as if to say: "Do what you will to me. I will match it."

Years after returning to the United States, Ruse would still recite a four page poem by Don Blanding that he had memorized while a captive in prison camps. The poem describes a home filled with the mostly exotic mementos its author collected in years of wandering the world. For the author, the house was but a wish and a dream. For my grandfather, it also served as a dream, a mental image and a fantasy to him and the prisoners who memorized it. It was a fantasy, but not fanatical. It was a tool to keep the mind sharp, and dually, it served as a source of hope in hopeless environs. He knew what happened to the men who had decided to give up hope. "You could tell it when you saw them. They would just go sit down and never get up again."

Memorization of such poetry was a way for the mind to pass the days between April 1942 and August 1945 when bombs dropped on Hiroshima and Nagasaki changed the world we live in forever (which he firmly believed had saved his life). As he put it in his later years, "I was always really fond of Harry Truman and his atomic bomb." Without it, would he have made it home to live out his POW daydreams?

When I have a house, as I sometime may, I'll suit my fancy in every way
And fill it with things that have caught my eye, in drifting from Iceland to Molokai…
It won't be correct or in period style but, oh, I've thought for a long long while-
Of all the corners and all the nooks, of all the book-shelves and all the books.
The great big table, the deep soft chairs, and the Chinese rug at the foot of the stairs.
It's an old rug from Chow-Wan that a Chinese princess once walked on.

He would later own a smallish three-bed, one-bath home with brown trim and a one car garage. Paid for by hard work in west Texas oil fields (and a booming post-war economy), it would be his home for over fifty years. There was a fishing boat in the back yard, a tool shed, and a carport with an old surplus army jeep that he took when deer hunting even into the last decade of his life. There was a porch swing in the front and one in the back with a fine pecan tree over head which kept family and friends supplied with pies for Thanksgiving and Christmas.

My house will stand on the side of a hill, by a slow broad river, deep and still,
With a tall lone pine on guard nearby where the birds can sing and the storm-winds cry.
And the door will squeak as I swing it wide, then welcome you to the cheer inside.

His grandchildren will all remember stepping up the two front porch steps to the door to the house. They would ring the bell, and listen for the heavy steps coming from the TV room around the corner where a football game was being watched. The front door would swing open, and he would look out the door, point to the youngest child he saw, and say "Who's *that?*" That would earn him a giggle, and they would step inside and take a pat on the back of the neck. The first order of business was a trip to the back bedroom and into a sock drawer in the dresser where one would fill his or her pockets with whatever candies happened to be in stock since the most recent trip to the members-only wholesale store, where it, among other things, was purchased and stockpiled in bulk.

On cold days, if he felt that one of these young guests was not appropriately outfitted for the weather, they would not leave the house without a coat on (nor would his adult children for that matter). "Dad never bought one jacket, but always three or four. He couldn't stand to think about being cold," said his son David. Even as a man of sixty, David would say he had probably never bought a coat on his own; his Dad was always giving a coat away. Cold winters as a POW with only a layer of thin and poorly-fitting denim had altered his sensitivities. It changed the way he used his senses. It changed the way he felt cold. It changed the way he felt hunger.

Cold was just one of many sufferings that he did not intend to endure again as long as he lived. He had lived through oppression, torture, starvation, beatings and slavery. As Ruse remained a hunter for many years, the house, over the years accumulated quite a gun collection. There was said to be a "gun at an arm's reach at just about any spot you could be in the entire house."

Vagabond House

When I have my house, I'll suit myself and have what I call my condiment shelf
Filled with all manner of herbs and spice, and curry and chutney for meats and rice,
Pots and bottles of extracts rare, onions and garlic will both be there,
Ginger with syrup in quaint stone jars, almonds and figs in tinsled bars,
Astrakahn's caviar, highly spiced, citron and orange peel crystallized,
Anchovy paste and pale jam, basil chile and mayoram,
Pickles and cheese from every land and flavors that come from Samarkand,
And hung by a string from a handy hook will be a dog-earred, well thumbed book,
Pasted full of recipes from France and Spain and the Celebes.
With roots and leaves and herbs to use for curious soups and odd rajouts.

When he parked his dodge pickup in the garage, the passenger had to get out in the driveway. There was no room to open the door. While this space was full, it was not cluttered. It was filled with canned food, hoarded and stacked to the ceiling. This was a man who was certain he would never go hungry again.

I'll go and my house will fall away while the mice by night and the moths by day
Nibble the covers of my books and the spiders weave the shadowed nooks.
And my dogs, I'll see that they have a home, while I follow the sun, while I drift and roam
To the ends of the earth like a chip on a stream, like a straw in the wind, like a vagrant dream.
And the thought will strike like a swift sharp pain that I probably never will build again—
This house I'll have in some far day - Oh well, It's just a dream house anyway.

Carl and Sara Ruse married in 1946 and lived in the same house for the rest of their days. All four of his children lived each of their childhood and adolescent years in the home, and he himself lived there until one day in 2003 he walked out the door to enter the hospital for an operation he would not awaken from. Sara had died from cancer in 2000, and he missed her greatly.

As a young man, home from war, he would rarely speak of his experiences, but when asked about his time as a POW, he told his story as a series of brave and hard facts with a brazen grit. Age, however, brought about a tenderness, and honesty that a younger man might not have permitted himself. He told his stories more, hugged longer, and did not bother to hold back emotions. When he ventured to give a complement to you, you could believe it because he had a tone of judgment that old age had given him. The sound in his voice, and square look in his eye left you with no doubt that he meant what he said, as if to say; "you should believe this of yourself forever."

After he passed away, his children went back to the house to clear out fifty years of living. His son filled the entire dumpster in the alley with food. "I would have tried to give it to the Salvation Army, but I don't think they would have taken it. Some of it had been in there for ten years or more." To a man who, at one time in his life, could count every decent meal he had had in a four year period on both hands, the date on a can did not mean much. He would not go hungry again.

In a drawer, a letter was found that was dated November 9th, 1945. The letter was from Sgt. Frank Harangody, who also recalled the poem, *Vagabond House*.

> *"Dear Carl:*
>
> *Thanks for your most welcome letter. I have often wondered how things were going with you. After you left Bilibid, and I'm happy that you came through, as I always knew you would.*
>
> *I have your letters that you have asked to be saved, and I'm enclosing them, including those of Lt. McCown, Have you heard from him?*
>
> *I was sorry to hear about your foot and your temporarily paralyzed right arm, but was happy to know that you are well on the road to recovery. I also hope that the Japs gave you plenty of Yasmay[a] out of the deal.*
>
> *Freeland made it O K and is at the Walter Reed Hospital in Washington D.C. As for me everything is all right, my new leg is working like a charm. I am now on a thirty day furlough, after the furlough is over the army will give me a verdict whether I can remain in the service.*
>
> *Of the boy's who are back, that I know of are Cobb, Devault, Rankin, Kolstad, Ammons, Huston, Clifton, Gillespie, Cambell, Walker, Bramely, Kope.*
>
> *Remember the poem the house by the side of the road. How true it was of the boy's over there, how they too made up their dream's of grandeur. And when they came back to the state's, I don't believe there are two that ever carried out their plans.*
>
> *Hoping to see you soon."*

At the close of the letter, it was signed *"Your Friend, Frank"*. At the bottom of the letter is a note in my Grandfather's handwriting. It read as follows:

---

[a] In Japanese, "Yasmay" is a reference to a "day of rest".

Vagabond House

"Frank Harangody was a Sgt. in my outfit. He lost both legs on Bataan. We were in Bilibid prison in Manila. When we went on to Japan he was kept in Bilibid with others who were unable to work. I had received some letters from my Dad. I left them with Frank because I knew the Japs would take them."[b]

Frank Harangody had gone on to become the mayor of Whiting, Indiana, and shared occasional correspondences with my Grandfather. While the "dreams of grandeur" described by the poet may not have come true, it seems that they did serve their purpose.

These men came home alive, and with intact minds. They came home to a world in which warmth, a full stomach, freedom, the ability to work for a wage, and life itself were truly grandiose dreams come true.

---

[b] Whiting Indiana is a suburb of Chicago on the southern coast of Lake Michigan.

Carl and Sara Ruse, 1946.

EPILOGUE

A STATUE OF RESPONSIBILITY

Youth may be admired for vigor,
but gray hair gives prestige to old age.

PROVERBS 20:29

Carl Ruse had been a prisoner for forty-one months and had worked as a slave laborer in the harshest of conditions for the entire time, except when being in the hold of a Hell-ship or while recovering from a broken leg received from the 1944 earthquake. For much of that time, not only were prisoners like himself slaves of the Japanese Military, but they were also used in Japanese companies that in the decades following the war became multi-billion dollar giants.

In June of 2000, an enormous lawsuit being considered by surviving POWs who had worked at the hands of Japanese corporations during the war made its way to a hearing in Washington D.C. The case was spearheaded by a few POWs who wanted to see justice for wrongs against them, and was taken up by an expansive legal team that had previously been known for such actions as suing tobacco companies on behalf of smokers.

For many POWs, this was an intriguing possibility to see justice happen in their remaining days. For the legal team, it was an interesting case with public support against some very large, profitable and well-known companies. I would imagine the dollar signs in their eyes could have been motivating factors as well.

Initially, the case had looked promising; however a 1951 Peace treaty with Japan prohibited lawsuits that would not honor the treaty. Secretary of State Madeline Albright received a letter from Senator Orrin Hatch, who had supported the case, and the reply he received was surprising: "We strongly believe that the United States must honor its international agreements, including the treaty," the letter stated. "There is, in our view, no justification for the United States to attempt to reopen the question of international commitments and obligations under the 1951 treaty in order now to seek a more favorable settlement of the issue of Japanese compensation." Following this, the United States Department of Justice filed a document that halted lawsuits pending judicial review.[1]

At the conclusion of the War, Congress passed the War Claims Act of 1948, which created a War Claims Commission (WCC) to adjudicate claims and pay out small lump-sum compensation payments from a War Claims Fund consisting of seized Japanese, German, and other Axis assets. Payments to POWs held by either Germany or Japan were at the rate of $2.50 per day of imprisonment.[2] Therefore, the argument was made that the POWs had already been compensated under the terms of the treaty.

In a hearing on June 28th, 2000, it was this treaty that the State Department cited in order to prevent further action. Senator Hatch responded by saying;

> "I can see how a government can waive its rights. I can see how it can enter into a treaty. I can see how it can do all of that. But what bothers me is how can [the government] without the consent of the individual citizens waive the rights of individual citizens who have been mistreated?"

We Volunteered.

The hearing ended with diminishing hopes of any progress against the Japanese companies. Former POW's slave laborers under Nazi Germany had been paid significant settlements following the war. This, apparently, was an impossibility for former prisoners of the Japanese. The government could waive its own rights by signing a treaty, but how could it wave the *rights of individuals*?

It had not been an impossibility for the United States to attempt to right wrongs against American-born Japanese families who had been interned during World War II. Out of intense wartime fear, approximately 120,000 Japanese-Americans had been taken from their homes and jobs and forced to build and live in internment camps for the duration of the war when President Roosevelt signed Executive Order 9066. However, when these Japanese-Americans sought the passage of a redress bill, the American government that came up with $1.25 billion[3] in reparations for these citizens who had been wrongfully interned during the war would not even attempt to compensate the POWs who suffered horribly to preserve that same government.[a]

An attempt at justice for Japanese-Americans had finally come, yet, that justice stung former POWs in that it only outlined the disparity in their treatment. Both the internment of Japanese and the inability of our system to protect those who have fought to preserve it serve as a reminder of the fallibility of our government. Yet, the patriotism of those former POWs such as Carl Ruse never faltered; they don't make them like that anymore.

In 2003, Senator Hatch had submitted what he called the "Justice for Veterans" amendment to the Department of Defense appropriations bill. This was a last hope to offer some sort of compensation to the POWs. The appropriations bill went through on September 17th that year; with no sign of Hatch's amendment. The POW legislation had been tossed out. Once again, the POWs

---

[a] On August 10, 1988 President Ronald Reagan signed the Civil Liberties Act of 1988 which authorized redress payments to Japanese families interned during World War II. In December of 1982, the Commission on Wartime Relocation and Internment of Civilians (CWRIC), a congressionally-created entity, concluded that the evacuation and incarceration of Japanese Americans during World War II were the result of "racism, war hysteria, and a failure of the nation's leadership." (Hatamiya 1993)

were sacrificed for what was judged to be the benefit of the public good.

II

As far as those close to him could see, Carl Ruse never felt that his country owed him anything. The Japanese military culture that assigned no value to human life, however, was a different story. As he might have told it, the debt they owed him was not one that could be paid; he was a creditor that could never collect. Even as a man matured into his eightieth year, Carl Ruse would turn out at Memorial Day ceremonies in his home town of Odessa, Texas to pay tribute to fallen soldiers from his war. After laying a wreath, he would stand up, back straight as an arrow, and salute his flag as crisply and with the precision of a guard in front of the Tomb of the Unknowns.

The reverence and sincerity with which he would take in the sight of his flag might stop you in your tracks; whether it be at a memorial service or during the *Star-Spangled Banner* at a Friday night high school football game. Having spent long years as a POW staring at another nation's flag overhead, the sight of the American flag *literally* meant safety and freedom to him. After those long years, a time came where he saw the flag for the first time and it truly represented safety to him; it let him know that from where he stood, he owned *freedom, liberty, and justice,* while, at the same time, his memories reminded him of what life out from under that flag represented.

In the fall of 2001, as an eighteen year-old home from college, I sat across from him in his living room as I had dozens of times in years past. At about this time, American flag stickers were common on the windshields of cars and in the windows of homes as Americans rode a patriotic high that came after the terrorist attacks of September 11th. While we talked, a news ticker scrolled along the bottom of his television, and his concern for our future was written on his face.

He looked over at me and said: "There will never be another time when this country is as patriotic as it was when I was in the service. I just don't think we'll see that kind of responsibility again." I didn't want to agree at the time, but he was certainly right. His generation, whether domestic or serving on a fighting front, *lived* in their war. Our citizens do not live presently in current wars, nor do we take such a sense of personal responsibility for them as did our citizens between 1941 and 1945.

A holocaust concentration camp survivor, Viktor Frankl, who loved the Unites States and what it represented, once said that the United States proudly displays a monument to freedom, the Statue of Liberty, on the east coast, but that this statue should be bookended by a *"Statue of Responsibility"* on the west coast.

Frankl said:

> *"Freedom is but the negative aspect of the whole phenomenon whose positive aspect is responsibleness. In fact, freedom is in danger of degenerating into mere arbitrariness unless it is lived in terms of responsibleness."*

Carl Ruse enjoyed a freedom that was not arbitrary. He had *personally* learned what it cost.

He died October 24th, 2003, only six months after the amendment requesting that POWs be acknowledged was removed from the defense appropriations bill. In the almost sixty years since his liberation, he had not heard an apology from Japanese government for the atrocities committed by their military.

An apology, however, was not something he sought, or expected. He was happy to be alive, and made a very productive life out of his free years. Like most other surviving POWs, his life would pass before a formal apology would come from the Japanese people. It was not until 2009 that an apology came from the Japanese Ambassador to the United States, on behalf of the Japanese people. By this time, only seventy three surviving POWs were alive and on hand to hear this apology. It was perhaps a sincere and meaningful gesture that was far from justice, which seldom follows war.

Six months after Ruse died, the National World War II Memorial was dedicated in a tranquil spot on the National Mall in Washington. The beautiful monument peacefully sits between monuments for Washington and Lincoln; a symbolically appropriate place for a memorial of a war that kept the efforts of both of these great leaders intact. I wish he had seen it.

Today, on the periphery of what was once the front lawn of Robert E. Lee in Arlington Virginia, new trees are being planted on flawless green hills that extend beyond the last rows of white grave markers. Their pale-green, thin leaves look alarmingly youthful next to the old oaks that have grown there for so long. Peaceful roads covered in the cool shadows of oak branches are extended out into the sunlight towards the newly-planted trees as if they are stretching their fingers into the future; a stirring reminder that our freedoms are an ongoing sacrifice.

Before his death, Carl Ruse had been offered a plot in the ever-growing Arlington National Cemetery. Perhaps taking a cue from his admired leader, Ed Dyess, he declined the honor for a final resting place next to his wife in his west Texas home town of Odessa.

He had lived a life that was a greater monument than bronze and granite. It was a life that in and of itself, was a statue of responsibility, not just arbitrary freedom; it was a life of earned freedom, bookended by an extraordinary responsibility.

AFTERWORD

Tell ye your children of it, and let your children tell their children, and their children another generation.

JOEL 1:3

We Volunteered was first published in August of 2010, and its publication brought about many contacts and friendships with people involved somehow in this story. A few months before publishing, while researching POW accounts pertaining to the prison camp at Ishihara-Sangyo in Yokkaichi, it had occurred to me that "the boy," (as my grandfather had called him) might still be living. As unlikely as it might be to track him down with only a photo and no name, I still had to try. The generosity and compassion of this boy in sharing food with my grandfather was significant not only because there was very little food to go around, but also because the caloric intake for a POW was so little. While I doubt that this ration of rice

183

was the difference between life and death, it certainly helped him along, and given that he weighed only eighty pounds at the time, it could have been.

In the Summer of 2010, I sent an email out of the blue to Kinue Tokudome, founder of "The US-Japan Dialogue on POWs" to ask for assistance in finding "the boy." She responded immediately, and quickly shared the story with a Journalist contact in Japan.

Kinue had become interested in POW issues as a Journalist following forced labor lawsuits of POWs against Japan, and ultimately came to befriend many of the plaintiffs in these lawsuits.

Thanks to Kinue's work, in early September, an article was published in the *Chinuchi Shimbun*, one of the largest newspapers in central Japan.[a] The photos of my Grandfather and the nameless boy were printed along with a plea to readers to contact the Journalist with any possible information.

After several days with no contact, a phone call came through. Father Shigeya Kumagawa, a peace studies teacher at a large Catholic boy's high school that was embedded into the Nanzan University in Nagoya had read the article and had been discussing it with his classes. Mr. Kumagawa also served as the Advisor of a committee made up of five students in the school who were given the task each year of choosing a speaker for the events commemorating the anniversary day of the school's founding. He contacted the journalist who wrote the article, who put him in touch with Kinue. I was surprised and honored to be asked by the students to come and share my Grandfather's story of a boy who shared his food with a POW. In the past, distinguished guests including Mother Teresa had been a guest for the occasion, and while I was flattered when being told this, I was proud that my Grandfather's story would be honored in this way.

II

Only weeks after receiving the invitation, my wife and I flew into Nagoya, where my brother Steve would be meeting us.

---

[a] http://www.us-japandialogueonpows.org/Ruse.htm

Arriving at the airport, I was met at the gate by Father Kumagawa and Kinue. On the train ride from the airport to Nagoya, Kumagawa and I were able to get acquainted, with Kinue serving as our translator.

I carried photos of my Grandfather and the boy in my hand, and showed them to Kumagawa, and answered his questions about my grandfather and our search for the boy. As he first saw the photo of my grandfather, I could see his face wilt with empathy for the suffering that the photo emanated. His posture deflated and he sank into his chair.

The photo of the boy, however, elicited a different response. As Kinue relayed more details of the story to him, I could see hope in him and pride in the story. Already I liked him, and wanted to know more about him.

Kumagawa was born just outside of Nagasaki in 1946. His father, one of eight siblings, was in frail health, and had been exempted from the draft. The rest of the siblings lived in Nagasaki and worked at a Mitsubishi factory, building weapons and machines for the war efforts. They lived in the district of Urakami in Nagasaki. Late in the war, as air raids were increasing, Kumagawa's father left Urakami and returned to their home village.

He had left just in time. When the atomic bomb fell on Nagasaki, twenty-six of Kumagawa's aunts, uncles and cousins were killed immediately. In their family, there were nine survivors who made it back to their mother's home after the bombing. In the following week, the remaining nine were dead.

The day after our arrival in Japan another article was printed in the local newspaper that told the story of our search and my visit to Nanzan. That morning I was able to share the story of Carl Ruse and the young man who had helped him, to an audience of over twelve-hundred students, as well as the Principal Officer of the US Consul to Japan. Our hosts were very gracious and the students were attentive and wide-eyed as they listened to the account of the story. Later that day one of them told me that he had had no idea of how POWs had been treated during the war, and especially in his own community.

We Volunteered.

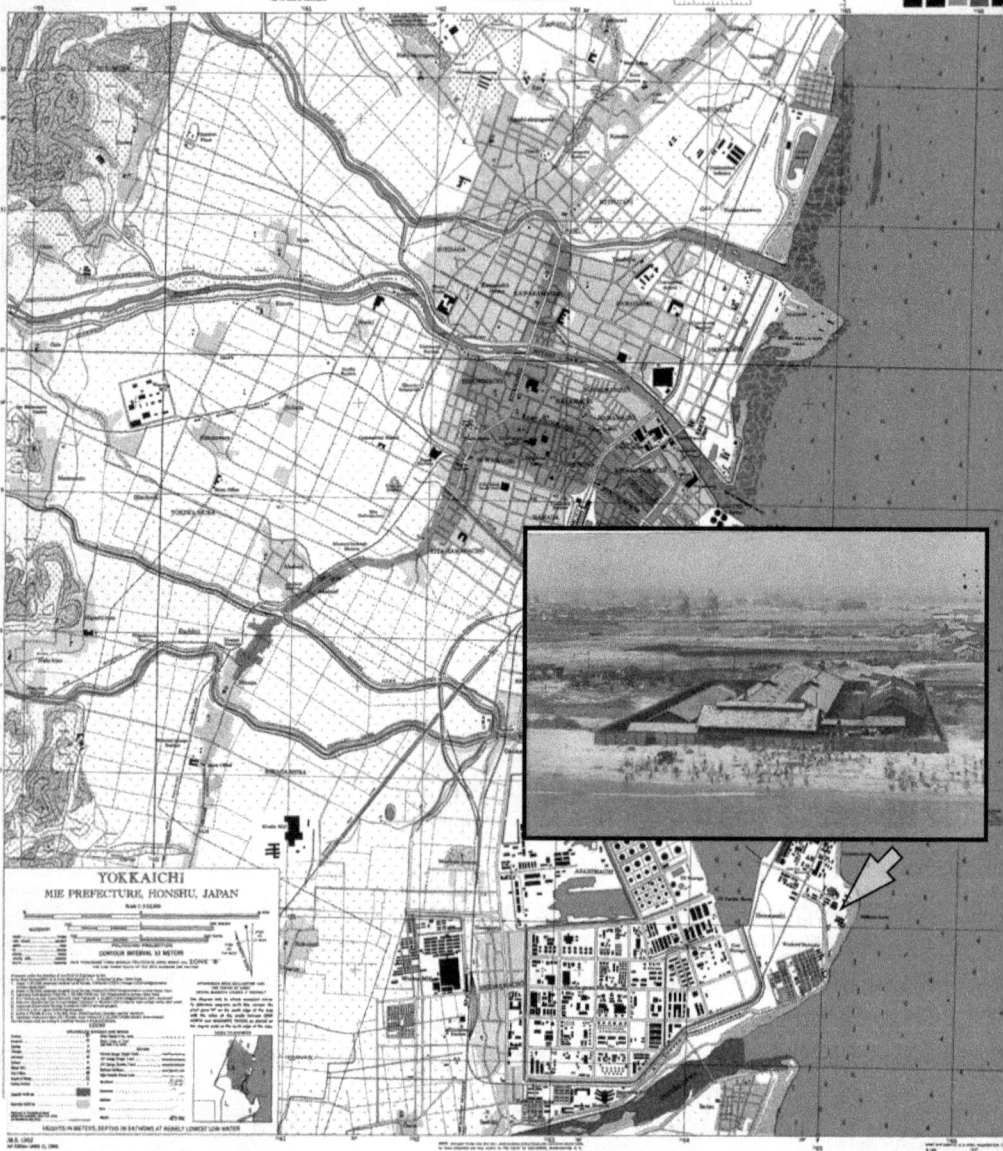

1945 Army Corps of Engineers Map of Yokkaichi. This map was used along with satellite coordinates to find the present day location of the prison camp, and the location on the beach where prisoners waved at Avengers flying over from the HMS *Indefatigable.*

186

The following day happened to be Veterans Day in the US. We spent it touring the factory of Ishihara Sangyo in Yokkaichi, where my grandfather had spent one year of his time as a POW. He arrived here on a train after two months in the hold of a ship that had come from the Philippines in 1944. We left Nagoya for Yokkaichi by train in the morning, traveling some of the same tracks that he had sixty-six years earlier. When we arrived in Yokkaichi, I was interviewed in a coffee shop by a reporter from a national Japanese newspaper, who accompanied us from that point forward.

After the interview, we left the coffee shop and television crews were already standing outside on the sidewalk waiting, and a van was parked outside to take us from the train station to the factory. When we arrived there were a number of Ishihara executives waiting to escort us inside. The staff at Ishihara had seen the original article that had been published two months earlier, and had been looking for clues about the boy we had been searching for, but had not had any success in tracking him down.

Nineteen prisoners of war died at the Ishihara Sangyo factory during the war. Steve and I laid flowers at a subtle garden memorial on the site before continuing to tour the site.

Using a 1945 Army Corps of Engineers Map of Yokkaichi with coordinates found along with present-day satellite images of the area, we were able to identify the location where the barracks had once stood where POWs had stood on the beach and waved at planes flying over and dropping food and supplies to them. It was amazing to stand in the place where he once stood, and I could imagine him looking up into the sky and seeing the planes flying over and knowing that his ordeal was over. He had survived and would go home.

Cameras recorded our visit to the factory as they had at Nanzan. Japanese news media emphasized our search for "the boy." We wondered if he would see the story or if someone would recognize his photo. Finally, on our last full day in Japan, I learned that Father Kumagawa at Nanzan had received a phone call. A man

187

who had seen the story on the evening news, believed that the boy was his deceased brother. Kumagawa arranged for a meeting with the man and his wife at our hotel.

We returned to our Hotel and were quickly taken to a meeting room and were introduced to Mr. Fumio Nishiwaki. Through a translator, he explained that his older brother had worked at Ishihara Sangyo as a young boy. His brother had described the smelter and working with American POWs. He even had once told him about giving food to a prisoner.

According to Fumio, Takeo was sent to work at the Ishihara Sangyo factory when he was a student at old Tomita High School. Fumio remembers that Takeo used to tell that he gave some potatoes to a POW from their family's farm. We also learned that Takeo's wife, was still living and had seen the photo and felt confident that this was a boyhood photo of her late husband. It had been fifty years since his death.

Nishiwaki Family. In this photo from approximately 1949, Fumio Nishiwaki is seen in the front row, 3rd from left. His older brother Takeo is seen in the back row, center directly behind Fumio. Photo Courtesy of Fumio Nishiwaki.

Mr. Nishiwaki produced a picture of his brother taken a decade after the one that we carried to Japan. He looked similar but it was difficult to be sure. Was this the boy that knew my grandfather?

Upon first seeing the photo, I was hesitant to believe that the boy was in fact the one whom we had searched for, but after speaking to Mr. Nishiwaki, the stories were very similar, and we felt that it was at least very plausible that we had found the one whom we were searching for.

At the same time, I thought of young Takeo, and in some ways, mourned his untimely death. My brother and I both agreed that, while there was some uncertainty as to the identity of the boy in the photo, that it was very significant that Mr. Takeo Nishiwaki had been in the POW camp at the same time, and he had done what he could to help some of the POWs who were there at the same time, and therefore his memory should be honored in the same was as if we had definitively proven to be the boy in our photo. I am very grateful for the Nishiwaki family for coming forward to speak with us as we were very enriched by having met with them. By coming forward, they brought more exposure to the story, and helped to lend additional credibility to the story among the people in Japan.

My Grandfather, while probably always burdened by an unknowable grief from what he experienced as a POW, saw an innocence in "the boy" that helped him carry on in life without the weight of bitterness that might have been expected. Being the recipient of compassion from an innocent child, he could not help but distinguish what he experienced as a POW from that of future generations of Japanese people. When he died in 2003, the photo remained in his wallet.

III

As we left our hotel in Japan, Mr. Nishiwaki met us in the lobby to say goodbye. I will never forget his words as we bowed farewell. "I'm going to go to the cemetery, and I'm going to tell my brother that we met."

INDEX

We Volunteered.

Works Cited

Bank, Bert. *Back from the Living Dead. Self-published. 1989.* Self Published, 1989.

Bartsch, William H. ""I wonder at times how we keep going here": The 1941-42 Philippines diary of Lt. John P. Burns, 21st Pursuit Squadron." *Air Power History*, 2006. Retrieved from URL: http://findarticles.com/p/articles/mi_hb3101/is_4_53/ai_n29316934/ (accessed March 1, 2010).

—. *December 8, 1941: MacArthur's Pearl Harbor.* College Station, TX: Texas A&M University Press, 2003.

—. *Doomed at the Start: American Pursuit Pilots in the Philippines, 1941-1942.* College Station, TX: Texas A&M University Press, 1992.

Bird, Kai and Sherwin, Martin J. *American Prometheus: The Triumph and Tragedy of J. Robert Oppenheimer.* New York, NY: Vintage Books, 2006.

Blanding, Don. *Vagabond's House.* Bedford, MA: Applewood Books, 1928.

Coleman, John S. Jr. *Bataan and Beyond: Memories of an American POW.* College Station, TX: Texas A&M University Press, 1978.

Craig, William. *The Fall of Japan.* New York, TX: Galahad Books, 1967.

Daws, Gavan. *Prisoners of the Japanese: POWs of World War II in the Pacific.* New York, NY: William Morrow and Company, Inc., 1994.

Dunn, William J. *Pacific Microphone.* College Station, TX: Texas A&M University Press, 1988.

Dyess, William E. *Bataan Death March: A Survivors Account.* Lincoln, NE: Bison Books, 2002.

Frank, Richard B. *MacArthur: A Biography.* New York, NY: Palgrave MacMillan, 2007.

Frankl, Viktor E. *Man's Search For Meaning.* New York, NY: Washington Square Press, 1946.

Goetz-Holmes, Linda. *Unjust Enrichment: How Japan's Companies Built Postwar Fortunes Using American POWs.* Mechanicsburg, PA: Stackpole Books, 2001.

Grashio, Samuel C., & Norling, Bernard. *Return to Freedom.* Spokane, WA: University Press, 1982.

Hatamiya, Leslie T. *Righting a Wrong: Japanese Americans and the Passage of the Civil Liberties Act of 1988.* Stanford, CA: Stanford University Press, 1993.

Works Cited

Heimbuch, Raymond C. *I'm one of the Lucky Ones: I Came Home Alive.* Crete, NE: Dageforde Publishing Inc., 2003.

Hubbard, Preston J. *Apocalypse Undone: My Survival of Japanese Imprisonment During World War II.* Nashville, TN: Vanderbilt University Press, 1990.

Lukacs, John D. *Escape from Davao: The Forgotten Story of the Most Daring Prison Break of the Pacific War.* New York, NY: Simon & Schuster, 2010.

McCullough, David. *Truman.* New York, NY: Simon & Schuster, 1992.

Miller Guinn, James. *A History of California and Extended History of Los Angeles and Environs.* Los Angeles, CA: Historic Record Company, 1915.

Morton, Louis. "http://www.ibiblio.org/hyperwar/USA/USA-P-PI/." *www.ibiblio.org.* 1953. http://www.ibiblio.org/hyperwar/USA/USA-P-PI/ (accessed June 3, 2010).

National Security Agency. "Mokusatsu: One Word, Two Lessons." *National Security Agency Technical Journal Articles.* 1968. http://www.nsa.gov/public_info/_files/tech_journals/mokusatsu.pdf (accessed June 3, 2010).

Norman, Michael, & Norman, Elizabeth M. *Tears in the Darkness: The Story of the Bataan Death March and its Aftermath.* New York, NY: Straus and Giroux, 2009.

Owens, William A. *Eye Deep in Hell.* Dallas, TX: Southern Methodist University Press, 1989.

Parkinson, James W. & Benson, Lee. *Soldier Slaves: Abandoned by the White House, Courts and Congress.* Annapolis, MD: Naval Institute Press, 2006.

Poole, Robert M. *On Hallowed Ground: The Story of Arlington National Cemetery.* New York, NY: Walker Publishing Company Inc., 2009.

Reynolds, Gary K. "Reynolds, Gary K. U.S. Prisoners of War and Civilian American Citizens Captured and Interned by Japan in World War II: The Issue of Compensation by Japan. Congressional Research Service: Library of Congress. 2002. Retrieved from URL: http://www.house." *Library of Congress.* 2002. http://www.house.gov/bordallo/gwcrc/RL30606.pdf (accessed June 3, 2010).

Smith, Jean Edward. *FDR.* New York, NY: Random House, 2007.

Tenney, Lester I. *My Hitch In Hell: The Bataan Death March.* Washington, DC: Brassey's Inc, 1995.

Tibbets, Paul W. *Return of the Enola Gay.* Columbus, OH: Mid Coast Marketing. 1998.

Whitman, John W. "US Army Doctrinal Effectiveness on Bataan, 1942; The First Battle." Thesis, US Army Command and General Staff College, Fort Leavenworth, 1968.

Young, Donald J. *The Battle of Bataan: A History of the 90 Day Siege and Eventual Surrender of 75,000 Filipino and United States Troops to the Japanese in World War II.* Jefferson, NC, 1992.

ORAL HISTORY

Ammons, Cecil. Interview by William H. Bartsch. April 1, 1980. Retrieved from the Douglas MacArthur Memorial Archives, Norfolk Virginia. June 21, 2010.

Ruse, Carl R. Oral History. Recorded by the Commemorative Air Force Museum, Midland TX. July 7th, 1999.

Ruse, Carl R. Interview by Bill Ruse. April 27, 2001.

Ruse, Carl R. Interview by Timothy Ruse. March 2001.

Ruse, Carl R. Oral History. Recorded by the Pacific War Museum, Fredericksburg, TX. January 23rd, 2003.

Works Cited

CHAPTER NOTES

PROLOGUE

1   Craig, 1967. Page xi.
2   Smith, 2007. Page 508.
3   Ibid. Page 510.
4   Bartsch, 2003. Page 95.
5   Craig, 1967. Page xii.
6   Smith, 2007. Page 519.
7   Ibid. Page 523.
8   Ibid. Page 510.
9   Ibid. Page 536.
10 Craig 1967, Prologue.

CHAPTER I

1   Miller-Guinn, 1915.

CHAPTER II

1   Dyess, 2002. Page 23.
2   Grashio, 1982. Page 2.
3   Bartsch, 2006.
4   Dyess, 1941. "Letter to Mrs. W.E Dyess"
5   Smith, 2007. Page 506.
6   Bartsch, 1992. Page 3.
7   Smith, 2007. Page 506.
8   Grashio, 1982. Page 2.
9   Dyess, 2002. Page23.
10 Hubbard, 1990. Page 22.
11 Ibid. Page 24.
12 Bartsch, 2003. Page 83.
13 Bartsch, 2006.
14 Coleman, 1978. Page 7.

15 Bartsch, 2003. Page 198.

16 Coleman, 1978. Page 7.

17 Dyess, 2002. Page 27.

18 Bartsch, 1992. Page 59.

19 Dyess, 2002. Page 30.

20 Bartsch, 1992. P age 73.

21 Ibid. Page 107.

22 Grashio, 1982. Page 8.

23 Bartsch, 1992. Page 121.

24 Frank, 2007. Page 44.

25 Bartsch, 2003. Page 393.

26 Frank, 2007. Page 46.

27 Grashio, 1982. Page 11.

CHAPTER III

1 Coleman, 1978. Page 15.

CHAPTER IV

1 Bartsch, 1992. Page 179.

2 Ibid., Page 180.

3 Bartsch, 1992. Page 180.

4 Dyess, 2002. Page 34.

5 Ibid. Page 34.

6 Bartsch, 1992. Page 123.

7 Dyess, 2002. Page 36.

8 Ammons, 1980.

9 Young, 1992. Page 15.

CHAPTER V

1 Norman, 2009. Page 93.

2 Whitman, 1968. Page 40.

3 Norman, 2009. Page 93.

4 Morton, 1953. Page 312.

5   Bartsch, 1992. Page 272.

6   Ibid. Page 243.

7   Bartsch, 2006.

8   Bartsch, 1992. Page 275.

9   Ibid. Page 275.

10   Ibid. Page 276.

11   Ibid. Page 296.

12   Dyess, 2002. Page 42.

13   Morton, 1953. Page 311.

14   Frank, 2007. Page 50.

15   Lukacs, 2010. Page 38.

16   Grashio, 1982. Page 17.

17   Dyess, 2002. Page 48.

CHAPTER VI

1   Bartsch, 1992. Page 375.

2   Frank, 2007. Page 52.

3   Norman, 2009. Page 149.

4   Ibid. Page 154.

5   Grashio, 1982. Page 38.

6   Bartsch, 1992. Page 376.

7   Grashio, 1982. Page 39.

8   Bartsch, 1992. Page 377.

9   Tenney, 1995. Page 37.

10   Grashio, 1982. Page 54.

11   Lukacs, 2010. Page 72.

12   Grashio, 1982. Page 55.

13   Lukacs, 2010. Page 73.

14   Ibid. Page 77.

CHAPTER VII

1 Grashio, 1982. Page 96.

2 Ibid. Page 96.

3 Ibid. Page 97.

4 Dyess, 2002. Page 149.

5 Grashio, 1982. Page 97.

6 Ibid. Page 100.

7 Lukacs, 2010. Page 116.

8 Ibid. Page 116.

CHAPTER VIII

1 Grashio, 1982. Page 101.

2 Heimbuch, 2003. Page 51-52

3 Dyess, 2002. Page 157.

4 Heimbuch, 2003. Page 72.

5 Ibid. Page 73.

6 Lukacs, 2010. Page 126.

7 Dyess, 2002. Page 120.

8 Lukacs, 2010. Page 104.

9 Dyess, 2002. Page 131.

10 Grashio, 1982. Page 124.

11 Ibid. Page 125.

12 Lukacs, 2010. Page 195.

13 Ibid. Page 196.

14 Grashio, 1982. Page 141.

15 Lukacs, 2010. Page 222.

16 Ibid. Page 198.

17 Bank, 1989. Page 26.

18 Ibid. Page 27.

19 Heimbuch, 2003. Page 66.

20 Bank, 1989. Page 27.

21 Grashio, 1982. Page 141.

22 Ibid. Page 166.

[23] Grashio, 1982. Page 179.

[24] Ibid. Page 180-181.

[25] Ibid. Page 183.

[26] Lukacs, 2010. Page 145.

[27] Daws, 1994. Page 281.

[28] Owens, 1989. Page 41.

[29] Heimbuch, 2003. Page 87.

CHAPTER IX

[1] Norman, 2009. Page 299.

[2] Heimbuch, 2003. Page 88.

[3] Ibid. Page 90.

[4] Ibid. Page 91.

[5] Norman, 2009 Page 305.

[6] Ibid. Page 301.

CHAPTER X

[1] Craig, 1967. Page 42.

[2] Tenney, 1995. Page 189.

[3] Craig, 1967. Page 29.

[4] Ibid. Page 45.

[5] Heimbuch, 2003. Page 92.

[6] Ibid. Page 94.

[7] Craig, 1967. Page 66.

CHAPTER XI

[1] Bird, 2006. Pages 314-315.

[2] McCullough, 1992. Pages 439-440.

[3] Craig, 1967. Page 66.

[4] Ibid.

[5] Ibid. Page 70.

[6] Tibbets, 1998. Page 234.

[7] McCullough, 1992. Page 457.

[8] Craig, 1967. Page 74.

[9] Ibid. Page 102.

[10] Ibid. Page 459.

[11] Ibid. Pages 118-119.

[12] Ibid. Page 126.

CHAPTER XII

[1] Ibid. Page 126.

[2] Ibid. Page 143.

EPILOGUE

[1] Parkinson, 2006. Page 75.

[2] Reynolds, 2002. Page 1.

[3] Hatamiya, 1993. Page 1.

www.ingramcontent.com/pod-product-compliance
Lightning Source LLC
Chambersburg PA
CBHW030759150426
42813CB00068B/3254/J